HELEN KELLER, PUBLIC SPEAKER

A few years before her death at age eighty-seven, Keller still displayed the vitality, vivaciousness, and vibrancy that contributed to her success as a valiant voice.

HELEN KELLER, PUBLIC SPEAKER

Sightless But Seen, Deaf But Heard

LOIS J. EINHORN

Great American Orators Series, Number 23
Bernard K. Duffy and Halford R. Ryan, *Series Advisers*

Greenwood Press
Westport, Connecticut • London

Library of Congress Cataloging-in-Publication Data

Einhorn, Lois J., 1952–
    Helen Keller, public speaker : sightless but seen, deaf but heard
  / Lois J. Einhorn.
      p. cm.—(Great American orators, ISSN 0898-8277 ; no. 23)
    Includes bibliographical references and index.
    ISBN 0-313-28643-4 (alk. paper)
    1. Keller, Helen, 1880–1968. 2. Keller, Helen, 1880–1968–
Oratory. 3. Blind women—United States—Biography. 4. Women,
Deaf—United States—Biography. 5. Women orators—United States—
Biography. I. Title. II. Series.
HV1624.K4E56 1998
362.4′1′092—dc20   95–41690
[B]

British Library Cataloguing in Publication Data is available.

Copyright © 1998 by Lois J. Einhorn

All rights reserved. No portion of this book may be
reproduced, by any process or technique, without the
express written consent of the publisher.

Library of Congress Catalog Card Number: 95–41690
ISBN: 0-313-28643-4
ISSN: 0898-8277

First published in 1998

Greenwood Press, 88 Post Road West, Westport, CT 06881
An imprint of Greenwood Publishing Group, Inc.

Printed in the United States of America

The paper used in this book complies with the
Permanent Paper Standard issued by the National
Information Standards Organization (Z39.48–1984).

10 9 8 7 6 5 4 3 2 1

Copyright Acknowledgment

All photos are reprinted with the permission of Helen Keller Research
Foundation.

Does not love—true love—suffer all things, believe all things, hope all things, endure all things? Love suffers long and is patient. It gives without stint, without measure and asks for nothing in return. It expects only good from the dear one through all trials and disillusionments. With such a love I cling to you. . . . You and I are comrades journeying hand in hand to the end. When the way is dark, and the shadows fall, we draw closer.

—Helen Keller

With love I dedicate this book
To my beloved Ana and Vaneza,
To my "adopted" daddy, Eric Loeb,
To the memory of my revered Teacher, Carroll C. Arnold,
And to my students—past, present, and future—
*   for whom I strive to be a beloved Teacher.*

"On Herself"

They took away what should have been my eyes,
(But I remembered Milton's Paradise).
They took away what should have been my ears,
(Beethoven came and wiped away my tears).
They took away what should have been my tongue,
(But I had talked with God when I was young).
He would not let them take away my soul—
Possessing that, I still possess the whole.
                                   —Helen Keller

Contents

Illustrations   xi
Series Foreword   xiii
Foreword by Bernard K. Duffy   xvii
Preface   xxi
Acknowledgments   xxiii

Part One
Visions of a Better Tomorrow:
An Analysis of Helen Keller's Speaking

Introduction   3

1 Rescued from Darkness: The Gift of Language   9

2 The World Seen Through Fingertips: Characteristics of
     Keller's Speeches   23

3 Just Because I Cannot See Doesn't Mean I Cannot Know   45

4 Not a Muted Voice: The Effectiveness of Keller's Speaking   71

Conclusion   75

Part Two
A Voice for Social Reform: Texts of Selected Speeches

Speech at Andover   79

Address of Helen Keller at Mt. Airy   80

Our Duties to the Blind   82

The Heaviest Burden of the Blind   88

The Conservation of Eyesight   91

The Gift of Speech   93

A New Light Is Coming   95

Menace of the Militarist Program   97

Strike Against War   99

Onward, Comrades!   104

The Vaudeville Circuit, 1919–24   106

Speech to Annual Convention of Lions Clubs International   109

Address to the Teachers of the Deaf and of the Blind   111

Commencement Address to Queen Margaret College   113

Address to the New Church of Scotland (Swedenborgian)   114

Address in St. Bride's Parish Church   115

Address to the National Institute for the Blind   116

Address to the National Council of Women   118

Speech to Knights of the Blind   119

Chronology of Selected Major Speeches   123
Notes   125
Selected Bibliography on Helen Keller   131
Index   151

Illustrations

Keller learning from Teacher through finger-spelling   2

The water pump in Tuscumbia, Alabama   10

Keller smelling a rose   46

Keller on the cover of Boston's *Home Journal,* 1896   47

Keller lecturing in public   76

Keller at 45 years old   121

A mature Keller still reading   130

Keller at 80 years old   150

Series Foreword

The idea for a series of books on great American orators grew out of the recognition that there is a paucity of book-length studies on individual orators and their speeches. Apart from a few notable exceptions, the study of American public address has been pursued in scores of articles published in professional journals. As helpful as these studies have been, none has provided—or can provide—a complete analysis of a speaker's rhetoric. Book-length studies, such as those in this series, will help fill the void that has existed in the study of American public address and its related disciplines of politics and history, theology and sociology, communication and law. In books, the critic can explicate a broader range of a speaker's persuasive discourse than reasonably could be treated in articles. The comprehensive research and sustained reflection that books require will undoubtedly yield many original and enduring insights concerning the nation's most important voices.

Public address has been a fertile ground for scholarly investigation. No matter how insightful their intellectual forebearers, each generation of scholars must reexamine its universe of discourse while expanding the compass of its researches and redefining its purpose and methods. To avoid intellectual torpor, new scholars cannot be content simply to see through the eyes of those who have come before them. We hope that this series of books will stimulate important new understandings of the nature of persuasive discourse and provide additional opportunities for scholarship in the history and criticism of American public address.

This series examines the role of rhetoric in the United States. American speakers shaped the destiny of the colonies, the young Republic, and the mature nation. During each stage of the intellectual, political, and religious development of the United States, great orators, standing at the rostrum, on the stump, and in the pulpit, used words and gestures to influence their audiences. Usually striving for the noble, sometimes achieving the base, they urged their fellow citizens toward a more perfect Union. The books in this series chronicle and explain the accomplishments of representative American leaders as orators.

A series of book-length studies on American persuaders honors the role men and women have played in U.S. history. Previously, if one desired to assess the impact of a speaker or a speech upon history, the path was, at best, not well marked and, at worst, littered with obstacles. To be sure, one might turn to biographies and general histories to learn about an orator, but for the public address scholar, these sources often prove unhelpful. Rhetorical topics, such as speech invention, style, delivery, organizational strategies, and persuasive effect, are often treated in passing, if mentioned at all. Authoritative speech texts are often difficult to locate, and the problem of textual accuracy is frequently encountered. This is especially true for those figures who spoke 100 or 200 years ago, or for those whose persuasive role, though significant, was secondary to other leading lights of the age.

Each book in this series is organized to meet the needs of scholars and students of the history and criticism of American public address. Part One is a critical analysis of the orator and his or her speeches. Within the format of a case study, one may expect considerable latitude. For instance, in a given chapter, an author might explicate a single speech or a group of related speeches or examine orations that compose a genre of rhetoric such as forensic speaking. But the critic's focus remains on the rhetorical considerations of speaker, speech, occasion, and effect. Part Two contains the texts of the important addresses that are discussed in the critical analysis that precedes it. To the extent possible, each author has endeavored to collect authoritative speech texts, which have often been found through original research in collections of primary source material. In a few instances, because of the extreme length of a speech, texts have been edited, but the authors have been careful to delete material that is least important to the speech, and these deletions have been held to a minimum.

In each book there is a chronology of major speeches that serves more purposes than may be apparent at first. Pragmatically, it lists all of the orator's known speeches and addresses. Places and dates of the speeches are also listed, although this is information that is sometimes difficult to determine precisely. But in a wider sense, the chronology attests to the scope of rhetoric in the United States. Certainly in quantity, if not always in quality, Americans are historically talkers and listeners.

Because of the disparate nature of the speakers examined in the series, there is some latitude in the nature of the bibliographical materials that have been included in each book. But in every instance, authors have carefully described original historical materials and collections and gathered critical studies, biographies and autobiographies, and a variety of secondary sources that bear on the speaker and the oratory. By combining in each book bibliographical materials, speech texts, and critical chapters, this series notes that text and research sources are interwoven in the act of rhetorical criticism.

May the books in this series serve to memorialize the nation's greatest orators.

Bernard K. Duffy
Halford R. Ryan

Foreword

Lois Einhorn's study of Helen Keller breaks new ground. Professor Einhorn proposed the book on Helen Keller while completing a book on the oratory of Abraham Lincoln, about whose inclusion in the series no one would cavil. Keller, on the other hand, might seem an unusual choice for a series on great American orators. Her speeches are not widely anthologized, and few critics have studied her rhetoric. But one of the benefits of the series is that it can serve to enlarge the canon of American oratory and raise to the surface figures who have been largely ignored. Thus far, the series includes books on other famous women orators—Elizabeth Cady Stanton, Frances E. Willard, and Anna Howard Shaw. In the blind and deaf community, few men or women became as prominent in their advocacy for the visually and hearing impaired as Keller. Although many have faced hardships rivaling Keller's, few had a story as well known as Keller's, and few had a voice as credible or as widely heard as Keller's.

But the celebrated story of Helen Keller's youth also fixed an image of Keller as a plucky, determined child who achieved a dramatic victory over what appeared to be insurmountable disabilities. The frontispiece of this book, a photograph of Keller in her eighties, will be far less recognizable than images that show her as a child with an outstretched hand, into which her Teacher, Anne Sullivan, insistently signed. The dramatic and memorable first act of Helen Keller's life has served to teach the lesson of persistence over adversity. The relatively unremembered second and third acts are, if less poignant, particularly worth the careful attention of rhetoricians. As an adult, Keller gave voice to her own story, revealing not so much her differences and her disability but the sameness and connectedness of her life with that of the sighted and the hearing. The hazards to Keller in embarking on a new journey as storyteller and sage, particularly at a time when there was less awareness of people with disabilities, were legion. It was tempting for audiences to sentimentalize Keller and for promoters to exploit her as a marketable commodity. Indeed, her appearance in circuses fulfilled that fear.

Professor Einhorn removes from mind the lingering image of the young Keller and supplants it with that of a mature, still highly tenacious woman who lived her life with vigor and courage. In her speeches, Keller grappled not only with the problems of her disability but with such issues as women's suffrage, pacificism, and the eradication of poverty. She was a reformer and agitator and member of the radical Industrial Workers of the World who preached the gospel of socialism. Those who disagreed with Keller were quick to blame Anne Sullivan, since Keller's radicalism was inconsistent with the sweetness of her youth, but in fact, Keller's ideas surpassed Sullivan's in their radicalism. In addition to her other struggles, Keller found herself a victim of the chauvinist desire to arrest women's intellectual and emotional development. Chauvinists and conservatives found the independent and free-thinking Keller, the woman, far less endearing that the romanticized, youthful Keller they had unhesitatingly admired.

Upon first reading Professor Einhorn's account of Keller's proclivity for archetypal metaphors, I wondered to what extent her repeated use of light/dark metaphors reflected her blindness. In keeping with the antithetical quality of her metaphoric usage, the themes of her lectures tended to be moralistic. It is fascinating to contemplate whether or not her radical ideology was also a product of her struggle against adversity. According to Kenneth Burke, the rhetorical function of language is embedded in the negative, that is, in the capacity of language to express moral proscriptions and prescriptions. Negatives, Burke argues, are first taught as "hortatory negatives" or "thou shalt nots," which form the basis for the expression of not being. In attempting to substantiate this hypothesis, Burke investigated Keller's unique experiences with language acquisition, finding that "the hortatory negative was taught first, and it was later applied for use as propositional negative, without explicit recognition of the change in application. Every parent of young children will report with dismay that the child's indefatigable desire to say *no* emerges almost as soon as the word is learned. One wonders whether or not Keller's extraordinary difficulty in asserting herself in a world that treated her as helpless might well have required her to nurture a radical aspect of her nature, which is manifest later in the anti-authoritarian, iconoclastic themes of her lectures. Another interesting question is the extent to which Keller's lectures were aimed at fulfilling the expectations of her audiences for testimonials and moral lessons, even though the specific lessons were not always the ones they wished to hear.[1]

Keller, who was remarkable for her adaptation to her disabilities, was also surprisingly unwilling to adapt to what those around her expected her to be and say. It is particularly appropriate that Professor Einhorn's revision of our thinking about Helen Keller focuses upon her words, for they were what united and divided her from others. It was, to the last, Keller's voice that made her independent and, in turn, her independence that made her great. Rhetoricians fondly tell the story of Demosthenes, the great Athenian orator, who overcame shyness and a lisp. Although Keller's oratory and influence do not match those of Demosthenes, her impediments as a deaf and blind woman were far greater. Within all of us, one would like to think, is the same spiritual call to fulfill the demands of the human character.

Professor Einhorn treats Keller with the sensitivity and perceptiveness that has contributed to her reputation as a teacher and scholar. She has published extensively on rhetoric and public address. For her book on Lincoln's oratory, she won the Everett Lee Hunt Award for distinguished rhetorical scholarship. For her teaching, she has received a panoply of awards including the Speech Communication Association's Donald H. Ecroyd Award for Outstanding Teaching in Higher Education, the National Speaker's Association's Outstanding Professor Award, and the Chancellor's Award, the State University of New York system's highest accolade for teaching. From this able scholar and teacher we learn much about Helen Keller, an uplifting orator who spoke from a unique vantage point for the cause of social improvement.

Bernard K. Duffy

Preface

I magine yourself living in a world of darkness and silence. It is black. Not dim. Not blurry. But totally black. It is silent. Not muffled. Not faint. But totally silent. It is not the darkness of having your eyes closed or the dusk of night but, rather, a deep, penetrating darkness. It is not the silence of covering your ears or the quiet of a tomb but, rather, the somber stillness of absolute and perpetual silence. You can see nothing. No sun. No snowflakes. No faces. Not even those of your family. You cannot hear a single sound. No laughing children. No music. No ticking clock. You cannot speak a single syllable. No "I love you." No singing even of "Silent Night."

You feel isolated from the outside world. Oblivious. Futile. Helpless. If a nuclear holocaust occurred, you would see or hear nothing, only feel rumbles, not knowing their source or meaning. You grope aimlessly in a terrifying world, void of oases or even of brief respites. You are wrapped up in a cocoon, but you do not like the solitude, the seclusion, the separation. You feel trapped.

You struggle without sight, sound, or voice to assist you. You not only hold things, but you hold on to things. You develop crude signs to signal your primitive wants. But, no matter how hard you try, you feel terrified, angry, and confused. You hunger to understand the world and to belong to it. You silently scream, but, of course, no one hears you. You stretch out your arms wildly in a panic, but no one reassures you. You feel lifeless. You are just an invisible presence, an unheard person, a muted voice.

This was Helen Keller's life prior to March 1887, when Anne Sullivan, her beloved Teacher and friend, arrived.

Then the eyes of the blind shall be opened and the ears of the deaf shall be unstopped.

—Isaiah 35:5

Acknowledgments

We all have "miracle workers" in our lives, people who help us accomplish our goals. I want to extend my genuine appreciation to the many miracle workers who have made this book possible.

First, I wish to thank Helen Keller, the subject of this study, who was my main miracle worker. Keller served as a source of constant inspiration by showing what happens when society shuts its eyes and ears, by asserting the sanctity of the soul, by championing just and honorable causes, and by giving visibility, voice, and vision to all humanity. One has to marvel at this miraculous human being who, although blind, deaf, and mute, celebrated the beauty of the world with all its sights and sounds. Clearly, her blind eyes saw, her deaf ears heard, and her muted voice spoke.

My own interest in rhetoric and communication was sparked by studying under some of the great teachers among teachers, including Carroll C. Arnold, Jerry Hauser, Dick Gregg, Herman Cohen, Gene White, Patty Andrews, J. Jeffery Auer, Jim Andrews, Bob Gunderson, and Dennis Gouran. Keller described her miracle worker, Anne Sullivan, in a way that accurately portrays my feelings for former professors:

> My teachers' genius and loving tact made the years of my education so beautiful. It was because [they] seized the right moment to impart knowledge that made it so pleasant and acceptable to me. [They] realized that a student's mind is like a shallow brook which ripples and dances merrily over the stony course of its education and reflects here a flower, there a bush, yonder a fleecy cloud; and [they] attempted to guide my mind on its way, knowing that like a brook it should be fed by mountain streams and hidden springs, until it broadened out into a deep river, capable of reflecting in its placid surface, billowy hills, the luminous shadows of trees and the blue heavens, as well as the sweet face of a little flower.

I am also extremely grateful to my colleagues and administrators at Binghamton University. They have consistently supported my research and teaching interests with knowledge, tolerance, kindness, graciousness, and humor.

I especially want to thank my students—past, present, and future—who make teaching a miraculous experience. To paraphrase what another teacher wrote: Two rewards of teaching seem virtually unparalleled. The first is the sense of extension I experience, as though I'm privileged to live inside one hundred different skins and to think one hundred different ways. The second is an offshoot of that: In no other profession can I feel repeatedly reborn to human life, in all the colors possible.

I extend my appreciation also to Bernard K. Duffy and Halford R. Ryan, co-editors of the Great American Orators Series, for having the foresight to create a collection of books on America's greatest speakers and for accepting Helen Keller as a speaker worthy of a book-length study. I am grateful to Mildred Vasan, senior editor of Social and Behavioral Sciences, for her assistance. I suspect that when this series began, the suggestion of such studies seemed like a "miracle."

Special thanks go to Judith Anderson, librarian at the Volta Bureau Library of the Alexander Graham Bell Association for the Deaf in Washington, D.C. Her generosity of time was obvious when she came in on a Saturday to open the library just for me! In addition, she provided me with a plethora of materials.

I thank Kenneth Stuckey, librarian of the Samuel P. Hayes Library of the Perkins School for the Blind in Watertown, Massachusetts. He is an encyclopedia of knowledge about Keller. I am especially grateful also to Carol J. Dollar, research administrator of the Helen Keller Eye Research Foundation in Birmingham, Alabama, for supplying me with the illustrations for this book and for sending me an abundance of information on Keller. Mostly, I thank Stuckey and Dollar for their generosity and for their enthusiastic support of my study.

My sincere appreciation goes, also, to Sue Pilkilton, director of the Helen Keller Birthplace in Tuscumbia, Alabama. Special thanks also go to Richard F. West, historian, District 22-C, Lions Club International, and to the main office of the International Association of Lions Clubs in Oak Brook, Illinois.

I extend my gratitude also to the many librarians at Binghamton University, especially those in Inter-Library Loan, Reference, and Circulation. They helped me in countless ways.

Helen Keller wrote, "Join the great company of those who make the barren places of life fruitful with kindness." I am eternally grateful to the many close people who fill the barren places of my life with kindness. My appreciation, admiration, and affection go especially to Vaneza and Ana, my precious loves, to the memory of Carroll C. Arnold, my Teacher, and to Eric Loeb, my "adopted" daddy, for their many kindnesses and unconditional love. I cherish the many miracles they have caused to take place within me, and I appreciate their teaching me that I, too, can be a miracle worker. I hope to make them proud.

PART ONE

Visions of a Better Tomorrow:
An Analysis of Helen Keller's Speaking

Keller learning from Teacher through finger spelling. Through finger spelling, Braille, the manual alphabet, lip-reading, and actually speaking, Keller learned about the outside world.

Introduction

I long to accomplish a great and noble task; but it is my chief duty and joy to accomplish humble tasks as though they were great and noble. It is my service to think how I can best fulfill the demands that each day makes upon me.

—Helen Keller, *My Key of Life*

From her birth in Tuscumbia, Alabama, on June 27, 1880, Helen Keller was a normal, healthy, intelligent, and active child. At nineteen months, an illness left her blind and deaf; shortly thereafter, she became mute. In her words, she was "less than an animal," trapped in a dark and silent world. At age six, Anne Sullivan became her teacher and constant companion. She taught Helen how to read, write, listen, and eventually speak. This ability to communicate emancipated Helen from the speechless silence and desperate darkness of her life. She felt reborn, filled with life and love. She became connected to the world. Keller's amazingly rapid progress and special talent for words attracted global attention. From the age of eight until her death in 1968, she was considered a "living miracle."

Keller was not the first or only blind and deaf person. In fact, a massive research study reported approximately 2,000 to 3,000 blind and deaf people in the United States and Canada around 1930. Why, then, did Helen Keller become famous while most of the others did not? In this book, I shall argue that Keller became famous, in part, because of her rhetoric. She earned her living by speaking and writing. They were her profession. In addition to sustaining herself, income from her speeches and writings supported the people upon whom she relied, such as Sullivan and Polly Thomson. Thomson lived and traveled with Keller, both before and after Sullivan's death.[1]

Keller spoke frequently, sometimes several times a day. She spoke on a variety of issues, including several of the social, political, cultural, and intellectual "hot topics" of the day. For almost fifty years, she purposefully used the gift of language, speaking all over the United States and world and writing several books and essays.

Although Keller spoke frequently and wrote many books and articles, there is a surprising dearth of scholarly writing on her speaking by rhetorical scholars. The *Index to Journals in Communication Studies Through 1995* does not list a single article on Keller published in communication journals before and through the year 1995. Perhaps the best sources of information about Keller as a speaker and writer come from Keller's rhetoric itself.

Many biographies of Keller exist, the foremost one by Pulitzer-Prize-winning author Joseph P. Lash. His book *Helen and Teacher* is an excellent biography, but it does not focus specifically on Keller's oratory. Two master's theses in speech communication examine Keller's socialist rhetoric, and one doctoral dissertation in English deals with representations of Keller. Although numerous books and articles have been written about her, no work focuses entirely on her oratory.[2]

This book fills the void. It concerns the public Keller, the ideas and images she presented to listeners at the time of delivery. The book combines rhetorical analyses of important aspects of Keller's speaking, texts of some of her important speeches, and an extensive bibliography.

In the analytical section, I argue that Keller was sightless but seen, deaf but heard. I begin by discussing how she learned to communicate, associating words with things, understanding abstract terms, and learning to speak.

Throughout her life, Keller made many comments about language, speaking, writing, conversing, and communicating. Chapter 1 collects these statements from her speeches, recorded conversations, books, letters, and other oral and written messages. In the chapter, I discuss how Keller credited language with rescuing her from the still silence that accompanies wordless sensations and with connecting her to the external world. She viewed language as a liberator, gift, and blessing, something to cherish and treat gently.

Chapter 2 discusses characteristics of Keller's speaking throughout her career, qualities that remained constant while a young girl and a mature woman. The chapter encompasses Keller's skills as a composer and a deliverer of speech. It examines how her style evolved from that of someone who could not speak to that of someone with little speaking experience to someone who became a famous public speaker. Keller is unique in allowing us to study this evolution from total isolation to command of large audiences.

Throughout Keller's life, some people have argued that she could not have written the speeches she gave because she had no direct experience about many things. For example, these critics charged, Keller could not have written about the color "red" because she had never seen anything red. Keller responded adamantly to these charges, defending her right to speak as an intelligent, thinking human being. In Chapter 3, I identify the criticisms levied against Keller and her responses. I also focus on how certain aspects of the criticisms and retorts relate to certain theories about the relationships between objects and words.

In the final critical chapter, Chapter 4, I examine Keller's effectiveness as a speaker. I examine how she was an effective speaker even before she opened her mouth because her very presence served as a symbol, a miracle people could see and hear. Added to her presence were her words of inspiration and hope. She raised huge sums of money for worthy causes and earned numerous accolades. Her impact as a speaker increased accordingly over time. She drew larger audiences, raised more money, and generally became known as one of the most unique women in history. This chapter examines not only *why* Keller was an effective speaker but also *how* she was an effective speaker.

Because Keller was considered a "miracle" from the age of eight, copies were made of some of her speeches. However, no book contains collections of her speeches, and in fact, *none* of her speech texts are readily available for study. Part Two of this book helps resolve this problem by providing texts of selected speeches, spanning time and topic.

Helen's first speech was a brief impromptu talk given in Andover, Massachusetts, in May 1891, when she was just ten years old. The speech concerned a young boy, Tommy Stringer, who was blind, deaf, and mute but whose family could not afford to provide him with a teacher. Through the speech and numerous letters, young Helen succeeded in raising enough money to support Tommy for over two years. Stringer attended the Perkins School for the Blind.[3]

Examples of Keller's early speaking career include the following: "Address at Mt. Airy," Pennsylvania, on July 8, 1896; "Our Duties to the Blind," presented in Boston at the Massachusetts Association for Promoting the Interests of the Adult Blind, January 5, 1904; "The Heaviest Burden of the Blind," given in New York City to the New York Association for the Blind, January 15, 1907; "The Conservation of Eyesight," presented in Boston at the Massachusetts Association for Promoting the Interests of the Blind, February 14, 1911; and "The Gift of Speech," delivered in New York City on April 8, 1913.

Most people know Keller as the spunky, intelligent child at the end of the film *The Miracle Worker*. Fewer people know that Keller was a socialist who actively advocated social reform. This book includes four speeches typical of her socialist years: "A New Light Is Coming," given in Sagamore Beach, Massachusetts, July 8, 1913; "Menace of the Militarist Program," presented to the Labor Forum at Washington Irving High School in New York City, December 19, 1915; "Strike Against War," presented in New York City, January 5, 1916; and "Onward, Comrades!" delivered in New York City, December 31, 1920. These speeches demonstrate a woman deeply concerned not only about the blind and deaf, but about *all* oppressed and marginalized groups.

From 1919 to 1924, Keller and Sullivan appeared on the Vaudeville Circuit. Keller prepared answers to frequently asked questions. This book includes a sampling of these prepared responses. Keller's retorts demonstrate her cynicism and her quick wit. To the question, "What do you admire most in your teacher," Keller responded, "Her sense of humor; her many-sided sympathy; her passion for service." Keller demonstrated these same qualities in her answers to the prepared questions.

Keller's speech to the 1925 International Convention of Lions Clubs International challenged the Lions to become "Knights of the Blind" in a "crusade against darkness." Lions Clubs International accepted this challenge. Chapter 4 details some of the many ways that Lions Clubs all over the world have served varying needs of the blind and visually impaired.[4]

In 1924, Keller began working for the American Foundation for the Blind. She talked to wounded soldiers in military hospitals and traveled around the world, giving inspirational speeches on behalf of oppressed people everywhere.

Keller could easily have given the same speech to different audiences. Instead, however, she adapted her speech topic and purpose according to the audience and situation. The following six speeches, all given in one trip, demonstrate this range and versatility: "Address to the Teachers of the Deaf and of the Blind," Glasgow, Scotland, June 10, 1932; "Commencement Address to Queen Margaret College," Glasgow, Scotland, June 15, 1932; "Address to the New Church of Scotland" (a church that shared Keller's religious beliefs in Swedenborgianism), Glasgow, Scotland, June 22, 1932; "Address in St. Bride's Parish Church," Bothwell, Scotland, June 26, 1932; "Address to the National Institute for the Blind," London, England, July 4, 1932; and "Address to the National Council of Women," London, England, July 7, 1932.

The "Speech to Knights of the Blind," Chicago, Illinois, 1953, illustrates the international nature of Keller's concerns. It also showcases Keller as a mature public speaker.

In addition to providing examples of Keller's speaking at different points in her life, the texts articulate the value she accorded the power of speech. They also allow you the reader to "listen" to her words yourself and to form your own interpretations.

In his biography *Helen and Teacher*, Lash wrote that the few archives containing primary source material on Keller have "never been used before by anyone outside of Helen Keller and a circle of intimates with a commitment to the Helen Keller canon." For this book, I visited and/or telephoned the directors of the four major research collections: The Helen Keller Archives of the American Foundation for the Blind in New York City; the Perkins School for the Blind in Watertown, Massachusetts; the Alexander Graham Bell Association for the Deaf (also known as the Volta Bureau) in Washington, D.C.; and the Schlesinger Library at Radcliffe College. I conclude the book with an extensive bibliography of books by and about Helen Keller for readers who want to engage in further study.[5]

The extensive bibliography on Helen Keller constitutes one contribution of this book. Since *none* of her speech texts are readily available for study, scholars who want to read Keller's famous speeches would need to visit or telephone the major research collections of materials on Keller discussed above. Providing the speech texts from these research collections in a book on Keller's speaking represents a major contribution to rhetorical history and theory.

This book on the rhetoric of Helen Keller provides insights into how she legitimized her right to speak as an able and intelligent woman. It also shows how she used the power of language to inspire. It identifies the many rhetorical achievements of this remarkable woman.

Without question, Keller was a *unique* orator of great reputation. She was unique primarily in being able to speak at all. She raised huge amounts of money, succeeded in getting government bills passed, and inspired the blind and the seeing, the deaf and the hearing, the mute and the speaking. Her evolved skills as an orator place her in the ranks of the most outstanding American women speakers of all time. Her achievements are undeniable. Her ability to communicate was largely responsible for making these things possible. This book on the rhetoric of Helen Keller contributes to our understanding of an important public person's acquisition and use of the power of speech.

In addition to providing the first thorough analysis of Helen Keller as a speaker, this book presents Keller as a life-like, not God-like, speaker, complete with strengths and weaknesses, consistencies and contradictions. It attempts to penetrate the Keller legend. Keller was a socialist, a pacifist, and a member of the Industrial Workers of the World. For the most part, Keller scholars either completely ignore her rhetoric dealing with these issues or attribute her unorthodox remarks to her concern with poverty as the leading cause of preventable blindness and her commitment to eradicating this affliction.

In this book, I argue that Keller's unpopular and revolutionary interests and ideas represent deeply rooted sentiments. They relate to her overall philosophy, as she expressed this philosophy in her rhetoric. Keller clearly presented herself as an unselfish woman with broad humanitarian interests. She was a woman with a mission. In her words, "I feel like Joan of Arc at times. My whole becomes uplifted. I, too, hear the voices that say, 'Come,' and I will follow, no matter what the cost, no matter what the trials I am placed under. Jail, poverty, calumny—they matter not. Truly He has said, 'Woe unto you that permits the least of mine to suffer.'"

To achieve her mission, Keller spoke and wrote to advance a vision of a better tomorrow. To her, a better tomorrow meant a perfect, pure, and peaceful period, a day filled with justice, equality, and love, a time when every human being viewed the entire world as one big family.

"What is a soul?" Helen asked Sullivan one day. "No one knows," answered Teacher. "But we know it's invisible, and it's the part of us that thinks, and loves, and hopes." Helen retorted, "If I write what my soul thinks, it will be visible, and the words will be its body." In this book, I shall attempt to analyze what Keller's soul thought as she expressed these ideas in her oratory. "Listen" to the speeches yourself and form your own opinions.

1

Rescued from Darkness:
The Gift of Language

Speech is the birthright of every child.

—*Helen Keller*

I shall learn to speak, too!

—*Helen Keller*

Throughout her life, Helen Keller credited her ability to communicate with rescuing her from the still silence and dull darkness that accompanies wordless sensations and with connecting her to the external world. Language was her liberator; it was a precious gift, something she always cherished. Her rhetoric contains a "well" of material for rhetorical scholars because she made numerous statements about words, language, speaking, writing, conversing, and communicating. In this chapter, I collect these comments from her speeches, recorded conversations, books, articles, letters, and other oral and written messages. To the best of my knowledge, these ideas have never been collected before.

To speak at all was virtually unheard of for a deaf-blind, mute person, making the fact that Keller became an admired and celebrated speaker all the more amazing. The uniqueness of her life provides the rare opportunity to follow the process of a human being's movement from a world of wordless sensations to a world where language functioned as the primary instrument of her success.

Before Language

Keller was born a healthy child. An illness at nineteen months left her blind and deaf. In later years she reflected on the period between losing her sight and hearing and her acquisition of language. She described herself as living in a "no-world" in a "time of nothingness":

The water pump in Tuscumbia, Alabama. The water pump still remains in Keller's birthplace home. It was here that young Helen connected the word *water* to the "cool something that was flowing over my hands." This incident represented the beginning of Keller's fascination with language.

Before my teacher came to me, I did not know that I am. I lived in a world that was a no-world. I cannot hope to describe adequately that unconscious, yet conscious time of nothingness. I did not know that I knew aught, or that I lived or acted or desired. I had neither will nor intellect. I was carried along to objects and acts by a certain blind natural impetus. . . . I never contracted my forehead in the act of thinking. . . . My inner life, then, was a blank without past, present, or future, without hope or anticipation, without wonder or joy or faith.

Keller underscored this sense of living in a void by continuing, "It was not night—it was not day" and by asserting that during this period she "had no power of thought." She referred to herself during this time of nothingness not as Helen but as "Phantom," a physical entity only purporting to be a human being but without the ability to think and communicate that, she claimed, makes a person truly human. In her book *Teacher*, Keller demonstrated the degree to which she the person differed from Phantom the thing by writing about Phantom in the third person.[1]

Like an animal, Phantom used crude signs to convey basic desires. For example, a pulling motion equaled "come," and a pushing motion meant "go." If she wanted ice cream, she pretended to turn on the freezer and shivered. She understood how to use a key and one day used it to lock her mother in the pantry! Although she possessed over sixty signs, she talked about how she still wanted to communicate; she wanted others to understand, and she craved the feedback that would tell her whether they understood. In the following passage, she discussed her sense of isolation, desolation, and desperation: "Ours is not the stillness which soothes the weary senses; it is an inhuman silence which severs and estranges. It is a silence not to be broken by a word of greeting, or the song of birds, or the sigh of a breeze. It is a silence which isolates, cruelly, completely." The degree of disorientation that Helen recalled experiencing appears to have been one of disjointed experience.[2]

Acquiring Language

Anne Sullivan, whom Keller affectionately called "Teacher," arrived in Tuscumbia on March 3, 1887, shortly before Keller's seventh birthday. For the rest of her life, Keller celebrated this day, calling it her "soul's birthday." The biblical imagery she used to describe this day highlights the importance she accorded it: "Thus I came out of Egypt and stood before Sinai, and a power divine touched my spirit and gave it sight, so that I beheld many wonders. And from the sacred mountain I heard a voice which said, 'Knowledge is love and light and vision.'"[3]

Because Sullivan recognized the importance of Helen understanding language, she immediately began spelling words into her charge's hand using the manual alphabet. For example, the blind children at the Perkins Institution, the school where Sullivan and later Keller trained, sent Helen a doll. When Teacher gave the doll to Helen, she spelled D-O-L-L into her hand. Keller quickly learned to imitate the letters in this and many other words, but she had no idea that she was communicating. To her the spelling was at first just a game. She did not yet understand the meaning of language.[4]

In her first autobiography, *The Story of My Life*, Keller described the now-famous account of April 5, 1887. Only a little over a month after Teacher's arrival, Helen stood by a water well and for the first time understood that words were names that represented objects:

> We walked down the path to the well-house, attracted by the fragrance of the honeysuckle with which it was covered. Some one was drawing water and my teacher placed my hand under the spout. As the cool water gushed over one hand she spelled the word *water*, first slowly, then rapidly. I stood still, my whole attention fixed upon the motions of her fingers. Suddenly I felt a misty consciousness as of something forgotten—a thrill of returning thought; and somehow the mystery of language was revealed to me. I knew then that "w-a-t-e-r" meant the wonderful cool something that was flowing over my hand.

It is difficult to think of an instance as dramatic as the transformation of Keller from an imitating animal to a thinking human being, or as Keller put it "from nothingness to human life." Referring to the word *water*, she said, "That living word awakened my soul, gave it light, hope, joy, set it free!" She had discovered what she called the "mystery of language." She considered this sudden ability to communicate a "mental awakening . . . an experience in the nature of a revelation." Whereas Teacher's arrival represented her "soul's birthday," this day, she called her "soul dawn."[5]

Physician and later novelist Walker Percy described this metamorphosis in a way similar to Keller's description:

> Eight-year-old Helen made her breakthrough from the good responding animal which behaviorists study so successfully to the strange name-giving and sentence uttering creature who begins by naming shoes and ships and sealing wax, and later tells jokes, curses, reads the paper, writes La sua volontade e nostra pace, or becomes a Hegel and composes an entire system of philosophy.

Percy called this breakthrough the "delta factor," named after the Greek symbol for irreducibility, something that cannot be reduced further. Keller's ability to communicate *did* represent the most basic element between her and the world; it allowed her to take the giant step between the mimicking animal and the thinking, communicating human being.[6]

Although Keller instantaneously learned that words were names, understanding many of the complexities of human communication evolved more gradually. In her book *Teacher,* Keller apologized to her readers: "Exceedingly I regret that in *The Story of My Life* I was careless in what I wrote about the progress Helen made in language and in learning to speak. The narrative was so telescoped that it seemed to ordinary readers as if Helen in a single moment had 'grasped the whole mystery of language.'" She continued:

> What happened at the well-house was that the nothingness vanished, but Phantom was not yet in a real world. She associated words correctly with objects she touched, such as "pump," "ground," "baby," "Teacher," and she gave herself up to the joy of release from inability to express her physical wants. . . . She only thought the words she had learned and remembered them when she needed them. She did not reflect or try to describe anything to herself. But the first words which she understood were like the first effects of the warm beams that start the melting of winter snow, flake by flake, a patch here and another there. After she had learned many nouns, there came the adjectives, and the melting was more rapid. Finally Teacher dropped in the verbs, one by one, sometimes in groups, but for Helen there was no connection between the words, no imagination or shape or composition. Only gradually did she begin to ask questions of the simplest kind. She had not conceived such things as "what," "where," "how," and "why," and other word-pegs and hooks on which we hang our phrases, but as she acquired them and framed halting questions, the answers from Teacher's hand banished her isolation.[7]

An additional step in Keller's acquisition of language was her ability to comprehend abstract terms. Keller recounted her struggle to understand the meaning of the word *love.* To her question, "What is love?" Teacher had responded, "'It is here,' pointing to my heart, whose beats I was conscious of for the first time. Her words puzzled me very much because I did not then understand anything unless I touched it." One or two days later, Teacher touched Helen's forehead and admonished her to "think." Keller recalled, "For the first time I knew that the word was the name of the process that was going on in my head. This was my first conscious perception of an abstract idea." With Teacher's help, Keller connected her understanding of the word *think* to her question about the meaning of the word *love.* She recounted her joy in learning about abstract ideas: "The beautiful truth burst upon my mind—I felt that there were invisible lines stretched between my spirit and the spirits of others."8

In reflection, then, Helen clearly understood that identifying and naming were not enough; the abilities to understand and to use abstractions such as "think" and "love" were essential elements of complex communication. True reciprocal communication required a comprehensive command of language—including its abstract terms and its connectives.

But Keller believed that one final step still remained in her acquisition of language—learning to use her voice, to speak. She noted that "the impulse to utter audible sounds had always been strong within me." Although the ability to communicate had liberated her from the still silence of wordless sensations, she still spoke about her voice as muted. She could communicate with the manual alphabet only with those who also knew the manual alphabet, which, of course, consisted of a limited number of people. In her speech at Mt. Airy, she explained how communicating only with the manual alphabet made her feel excluded and secluded: "I can remember the time before I learned to speak and how I used to struggle to express my thoughts by means of the manual alphabet—how my thoughts used to beat against my finger tips like little birds striving to gain their freedom." Speaking was also important to her sense of self: "'Without a language of some sort, one is not a human being; without speech one is not a complete human being.'"9

In 1890, a teacher of Laura Bridgman, the first deaf-blind child to receive a systematic education, returned from abroad and told Keller and Teacher about a deaf-blind girl in Norway who had learned to speak. When Helen heard the news, she exclaimed enthusiastically, "'I shall learn to speak, too!'" And she did. She persuaded Teacher to take her to the Horace Mann School in Boston where she studied under the principal, Miss Sarah Fuller. By lightly touching Fuller's face, Keller felt the position of the lips and tongue in making different sounds and then imitated these sounds herself. The process was slow, tedious, laborious, and difficult, but Keller was determined and persisted. "I shall never forget," she recalled, "the surprise and delight I felt when I uttered my first connected sentence, 'It is warm.' True, they were broken and stammering syllables; but they were human speech. My soul, conscious of new strength, came out of bondage, and was reaching through those broken symbols of speech to all knowledge and all faith." Keller continued her quest to speak like seeing and hearing people. In 1894, she went to the Wright-Humason School for the Deaf in New York City to continue her training in speaking and lipreading. Alexander Graham Bell, one of her lifelong supporters, also gave her some private lessons in articulation.10

By learning to speak, Keller took a stance in an ongoing controversy among members of the deaf community: Should deaf people learn to speak, or should they learn to use sign language? By becoming an oralist, Keller could not communicate with deaf people who knew only sign language. Not surprisingly, some of these deaf people felt offended. In an effort to alienate no one, Keller wrote an article in the *American Annals of the Deaf,* a publication published and read primarily by people who took the sign language side in the speaking versus sign language controversy. In the article, Keller wrote, "No method is perfect. I realize that I have had exceptional advantages . . . skillful teaching and the constant, watchful care of devoted friends to keep my speech intelligible." She articulated what she considered the underlying issue: What would help deaf people most to feel included rather than isolated? She admitted, "Without the sign language, many hundreds of deaf people would be isolated."[11]

Despite Keller's diligent and frequent practice, she never succeeded in reaching her goal of speaking so everyone could understand all her words. In listening to a few audio recordings of Keller's voice and watching a few clips of her speeches on television, I can understand most of what she says, but only if I work extremely hard at listening carefully. Even then, however, I do not grasp every word. People who heard Keller speak in public described her voice as coarse, grainy, and harsh in sound; variety in rate, volume, pitch, and emphasis was virtually nonexistent. Hence, Keller was understood completely by those who knew her well but only a little by those in her audience. In later years, she identified the cause of her failure—she and her teachers, she said, "had tried to build up speech without voice production!" They should have developed her vocal organs first and only afterwards taught her articulation.[12]

Still, Keller's ability to speak at all brought her enormous hope and joy and bolstered her sense of self. She concluded her speech at Mt. Airy by exclaiming about all deaf children, "Sometime, somewhere, somehow we shall find that which we seek. We shall speak, yes, and sing, too, as God intended we should speak and sing." Just as Keller's description of Teacher's arrival contained biblical imagery, so did her description of her learning to speak, again emphasizing its import to her: "It was as if Isaiah's prophecy had been fulfilled in me, 'The mountains and the hills shall break forth before you into singing, and all the trees of the field shall clap their hands!'" And regarding her identity, Keller remarked, "With the acquisition of speech, I moved from the baby phase of my mental growth to my identity as a separate, conscious, and to a degree, self-determining ego."[13]

The Effects of Acquiring Language

Because of language, Keller could, and did, think, converse with others, speak publicly, write letters, articles, and books, and read the great works of others. Language was so important to how she thought of herself as a person that her discourse included many discussions of the effects of acquiring language. The development of language served several functions in her life. It made her feel alive, connected her to other people, helped her to "see" and "hear" things she could not actually see or hear, emancipated her, and allowed her to feel equal to people with all their faculties. Language also provided her with a way to have fun, corresponded with her moral concerns, and provided her a unique role in life.

Keller frequently spoke about how language made her feel alive. For example, about connecting the word *water* to the object, she said, "That living word awakened my soul." During the rest of that day, she touched many objects, eager to learn their names. Everything she touched, she said, "seemed to quiver with life." Keller often used the word *living* as an adjective as in "living word" in the example above or "living words" in her address at Mt. Airy: "I cannot understand how any one interested in our education can fail to appreciate the satisfaction we feel in being able to express our thoughts in *living* words" (emphasis added). Using *living* in this way suggests that she viewed words as alive and believed that using words made the speaker alive.[14]

Language functioned to link Keller to other people. Through the manual alphabet, Braille, lipreading, and actually speaking, she wrote, read, listened, and spoke. She read aloud, told stories, and discussed the political issues of the day. In her speech at Mt. Airy, she explained, "So you see what a blessing speech is to me. It brings me into closer and tenderer relationship with those I love, and makes it possible for me to enjoy the sweet companionship of a great many persons from whom I should be entirely cut off if I could not talk."

Keller depended on language to construct her reality for things requiring the ability to see or hear. If she could not physically experience something, she accepted descriptions from Teacher or other people. Linguistic constructs were as real to her as the things she experienced with her own senses. Thus, language allowed Keller to "see" and to "hear."

Language also functioned to emancipate Keller. Her many discourses on language often included the metaphors of slavery and captivity. Without language, she described herself as a "captive," in "bondage," and "imprisoned." Likewise, she used the language of deliverance when discussing her ability to communicate, especially the words *liberty* and *freedom*. Keller almost always associated the lack of communication with *darkness, night, pessimism,* and *silence* and the ability to communicate with *light, day, optimism, love, hope,* and *joy.* The following is a typical passage: "Once I knew the depth where no *hope* was, and *darkness* lay on the face of all things. Then *love* came and set my soul *free.* . . . *Night* fled before the *day* of thought, and *love* and *joy* and *hope* came up in a passion of obedience to knowledge. Can any one who has escaped such *captivity,* who has felt the thrill and glory of *freedom,* be a *pessimist* [emphases added]?" Captivity to Keller equaled ignorance, while freedom equaled knowledge.

Knowledge, to Keller, was very important. She likened it to religion, remarking, "Knowledge is holy ground." She also claimed that knowledge equaled power and happiness:

> "Knowledge is power." Rather, knowledge is happiness, because to have knowledge—broad, deep knowledge—is to know true ends from false, and lofty things from low. To know the thoughts and deeds that have marked man's progress is to feel the great heart-throbs of humanity through the centuries; and if one does not feel in these pulsations a heavenward striving, one must indeed be deaf to the harmonies of life.[15]

Language made Keller equal to people who could see and hear. With books especially, she was neither blind nor deaf. The knowledge or wisdom of the ages found in books connected her to humanity's past, present, and future. She called books her "friends," explaining, "In a word literature is my Utopia. Here I am not disenfranchised. No barrier of the senses shuts me out from the sweet, gracious discourse of my book-friends." Unlike people, books could not feel tired, troubled, embarrassed, or awkward. Books, then, equaled normalcy and deliverance. When reading she could retreat, flee freely, and have a furlough from her circumscribed world.[16]

Keller also used language as a way to have fun. She was especially fond of conundrums, riddles whose answers turn on a play of words. The conundrums below are typical:

> My first is a body of water; my second is an exclamation; my third is used in fishing—BAYONET [bay o net].
>   Why can I not spell *cupid?* Because when I C U [I see you] I can go no farther.[17]

Keller often used a play of words to answer interview questions in a way that sometimes resulted in biting humor. For example, while on the Vaudeville Tour in 1919, Warren Harding was president. When asked, "What do you think of Mr. Harding?" Keller responded, "I have a fellow feeling for him; he seems as blind as I am."

Language provided Keller with a profession. Her love of words and her literary talents coupled with the curiosity of a national and international public made speaking and writing natural outlets for her to share her unique experiences. From the age of eight, she was considered a "living miracle." Her special talent for words was part of what attracted global attention. Keller spoke and wrote for a career, and she became famous in part because of her ability to speak and write.

Finally, Keller's education and her social and political views allowed her to use language as an instrument for moral and political commentary. As I shall discuss in the next chapter, the core of her being wanted to make the world a better place. "Somehow," she remarked, "I cannot make myself care very much whether two and two make four or five because I cannot see that the knowledge of these facts makes life any sweeter or nobler." The ability to communicate, however, made life both sweeter and nobler. The chance to speak, she contended, equaled the chance to better oneself in life, which was a central theme of her rhetoric. In her speech "The Gift of Speech," she declared that "speech is the birthright of every child" and that all children deserve access to the knowledge that speech allows. With speech comes responsibility: Those who possess the power of speech, she argued, have the moral obligation to use their knowledge prudently and to try to attain this power for all. She eloquently elaborated on how all people need to nourish humanity with this "bread of knowledge." She began by explaining that "deafness is a greater disaster than blindness" because "[b]lindness robs the day of its light and makes us physically helpless," while "[d]eafness stops up the fountain-head of knowledge and turns life into a desert. For without language, intellectual life is impossible." She appealed to her listeners with the plea, "We must not wait for the deaf to ask for speech. . . . We who see, we who hear, we who understand must help them, must give them the bread of knowledge, must teach them what their human inheritance is." Significantly, Keller included herself as part of the "we who see" and the "we who hear" because she possessed the ability to communicate and, thus, to engage in intellectual life.[18]

Keller's Education

A general aura of idealism informed Keller's education at almost all stages, in part because Sullivan possessed strong idealistic and moral views and because her teaching methods were unique, especially for the time. Rather than focusing on her pupil's handicaps, Teacher educated her charge just as she would have educated a sighted and hearing child. In her words, "I asked myself, *'How does a normal child learn language?'* The answer was simple. 'By imitation.'" Observing Helen's fifteen-month-old cousin gave Teacher "a clue to the method to be followed in teaching Helen language. *I shall use complete sentences in talking to her,* and fill out the meaning with gestures and her descriptive signs when necessity requires it."[19]

Teacher also adamantly argued that for the first few years Helen would learn more by *not* following a systematic curriculum. She criticized traditional educational methods, contrasting them with her ideas:

> Apparently, children learn language more quickly when they are free to move about among objects that interest them. They absorb words and knowledge simultaneously. In the class-room they cease to be actors in the drama; they sit and watch the teacher doing something with her mouth which does not excite their curiosity particularly. . . . The contrast between these children's plodding pursuit of knowledge and Helen's bounding joyousness makes me wonder.

To Helen, learning seemed like play. Most "lessons" took place outdoors because Helen, like other children, was especially interested in living things such as animals, trees, and flowers. She wrote, "Indeed, everything that could hum, or buzz, or sing, or bloom, had a part in my education." It is no exaggeration to say that she went to Schoolhouse Earth.[20]

From the beginning, Teacher insisted that Helen phrase her ideas correctly and in complete sentences. Keller explained the process used:

> As soon as I could spell a few words my teacher gave me slips of cardboard on which were printed words in raised letters. I quickly learned that each printed word stood for an object, an act, or a quality. I had a frame in which I could arrange the words in little sentences; but before I ever put sentences in the frames I used to make them in objects. I found the slips of paper which represented, for example, "doll," "is," "on," "bed" and placed each name on its object; then I put my doll on the bed with the words *is, on, bed* arranged beside the doll, thus making a sentence of the words, and at the same time carrying out the idea of the sentence with the things themselves.[21]

The combination of Sullivan's teaching methods, Keller's retentive memory and insatiable curiosity, and the discipline and determination of both Teacher and pupil helped Keller to learn very quickly. In a short period of time, her vocabulary increased and her communication became remarkably fluent, rich, and detailed for a child her age. The following journal entries written by Helen at age seven demonstrate the facility she had with words:

Jan. 9, 1888 Apples have no edges and no angles. Apples grow on trees. They grow in orchards. When they are ripe they fall on the ground.

March 1, 1888 Oranges look like golden apples hanging on the trees. They have a thick skin, and inside is the sweet juicy pulp and seeds. All boys and girls like oranges to eat. Bananas have a thick, smooth skin, and hang on trees in long branches. . . . I learned what view means. People can view trees and flowers and grass and hills and sky is view.

In May 1888, it was determined that a more systematic educational approach would now be in Helen's best interests. So, she and Teacher went to the Perkins Institution in Boston. In 1894, Keller attended the Wright-Humason School for the Deaf in New York, and in 1896, she studied at the Cambridge School for Young Ladies in Cambridge, Massachusetts. All of her informal and formal schooling prepared her for college. She graduated cum laude from Radcliffe College in 1904 with honors in English and German. By this time she also knew some French, Greek, and Latin. All of Keller's education encouraged her to devote her life to the study and use of language.

Summary and Conclusions

Helen Keller had the extraordinary experience of changing from a mimicking animal to an active, thinking human being. The acquisition of language caused this transmutation. Few people remember learning language. Keller's life is unique in allowing us to follow her transformation and her explanation of the entire process—before learning language, learning language, and after learning language. Before possessing the ability to communicate, Keller described herself as "Phantom," an imitating animal who could not think. After her experience at the wellhouse, she became a thinking human being, linked to all humanity.

Keller explained her acquisition of language as occurring in four steps. First, at the well-house, she instantly received the ability to communicate and, thus, to think. Second, she gradually learned about the complexities of human communication. Third, she understood things she could not touch including abstract terms and emotions. Finally, she learned to speak. Thinking, communicating with her fingers, feeling, and speaking with her voice linked Keller to the world of people and ideas.

For centuries scholars have debated whether people can think without words. Keller's rhetoric on her acquisition of language says no: She argued that she could not think until she discovered language. Before her experience at the well-house, she described herself as an imitating animal who could not think. Only when she learned the meaning of language, she contended, could she engage in rational thought processes.

As we shall learn in the next chapter, Keller argued that ignorance created a blindness and deafness more dangerous than the absence of eyesight and hearing. She expressed surprise and outrage that many sighted and hearing people were blind and deaf to the conditions of humankind, and she often used "blindness" and "deafness" as metaphors. For example, she remarked, "My darkness had been filled with the light of intelligence and, behold, the outer daylit world was stumbling and groping in social blindness!" In numerous ways and at numerous times, she contended that communication and education could solve the problems of social blindness and deafness. Her rhetoric contains frequent pleas for serious study, educated exchanges, patient propositions, careful choices, informed ideas, responsible reasons, and conscientious changes. For example, in the peroration of "The Gift of Speech," she artfully argued that giving all people the chance to speak would lessen the social blindness and deafness in the world: "Let us here and now resolve that every deaf child shall have a chance to speak, and that every man shall have a fair opportunity to make the best of himself. Then shall we mend the broken lyre of human speech and lessen the deafness and blindness of the world." Given the importance of communication and education in her own life, it is not surprising that she viewed them as solutions to the world's problems. In the next chapter, I shall discuss Keller's "visions" for a better tomorrow and explain how she tried to help people see the world's problems in a new "light."[22]

2

The World Seen Through Fingertips: Characteristics of Keller's Speeches

Because Helen Keller spoke for almost eighty years and because she concerned herself with so many issues, her speaking shows considerable range. She spoke frequently, sometimes several times a day. She earned her living by speaking and writing. She spoke with the Chautauqua lecture circuit, a group consisting primarily of professional lecturers; made a film in Hollywood; and took part in a vaudeville tour. She repeatedly went on speaking tours in the United States, Europe, Asia, Africa, and Latin America.

In this chapter, I discuss characteristics of Keller's speeches, qualities of her speaking that remained constant throughout her years as a young girl and as a mature woman. In addition, I examine the evolution of Keller's speaking from that of a peaceful persuader to an able advocate to a radical reformer to, in Eleanor Roosevelt's words, "a goodwill ambassador of the United States."[1]

Characteristics of Keller's Speeches

Keller frequently talked about personal topics the public wanted to know about such as what her life was like, how she learned language, and how she dreamed. She spoke also about personal interests such as religion, mysticism, and extrasensory perception. But the depth of her knowledge and the breadth of her concerns resulted in her speaking also on a variety of humanitarian issues, including many of the hot topics of the day. Among the many causes she championed, she spoke *for* reforms affecting the blind and deaf, rights for workers, women's suffrage, pacifism, socialism, and birth control, and she spoke *against* poverty, child labor, the capitalist system, and capital punishment.

Even as a young girl, Keller talked about wanting her lifework to involve *making a difference.* Lack of freedom, justice, and equality stirred her to speak. Much of her rhetoric concerned empowering oppressed, suppressed, disenfranchised, and marginalized groups and classes, which, she maintained, constituted the vast majority of people. Keller identified with these burden bearers. She was a humanitarian in the truest sense, always concerned with actively helping to improve the welfare of humankind.

Keller demonstrated her humanitarian heart even as a young child. When she was ten years old, she learned about Tommy Stringer, a deaf-blind and mute child, like herself. Unlike Helen, however, Tommy's mother was dead, and his father did not have the money to hire a tutor. When Helen pleaded with people to help Tommy, she was told that teachers like Anne Sullivan cost a lot of money. Helen instantly replied, "We will raise it." And she did. In her first fund-raising campaign, she collected over $1,600. Most of this money came from her request to people who offered to give her money to buy a dog to replace the dog of hers that had recently been killed. Helen requested that these people contribute, instead, to a fund for Tommy's education. As she explained in one letter, this plan would "help make Tommy's life as bright and joyous as mine. . . . Education will bring light and music into Tommy's soul, and then he cannot help being happy."[2]

A Rhetoric of Strong Conflicts

Keller's correspondence about Tommy Stringer reveals the innocent, idyllic worldview of young Helen. In her girlhood speeches and writings, she talked about *all* people as good, and she described *everything* in her life as joyous. Initially, through her inner eyes, the world was perfect, pure, and peaceful. Other people also have made this observation. For example, Lash has written that when Helen was young, "[s]he was already showing a tendency to modify the facts about—even to block out—the violent, the disgusting and the distasteful." Perhaps the fact that those closest to Helen described her as a consummate example of a magnanimous, benevolent person furthered her tendency to see the world only in positive ways. Teacher wrote, "I do not believe that a selfish or unkind word ever entered her head." Anagnos, the director at Perkins, described Helen similarly: "It is no hyperbole to say that she is a personification of goodness and happiness." He continued, "Of sin and evil, of malice and wickedness, of meanness and perverseness, she is absolutely ignorant. She is as pure as the lily of the valley, and as innocent and joyous as the birds of the air or the lambs in the field. No germ of depravity can be detected in the soul of her moral constitution, even by means of the most powerful microscope."[3]

As she matured and interacted more with people outside of her extended family, Keller encountered evil and pictured the world in her speeches and writings as a conflict between good and evil, right and wrong, God and the devil, light and darkness. Her worldview, as she described it, held no place for ambiguity or a middle ground. Helen recalled when she recited to Teacher an ode from Horace. Teacher declared, "Horace is right, Helen. There are few things you can absolutely call black or white." But Helen rejected Teacher's point, explaining that she could not understand "any middle between good and evil." She continued, "This is a contradiction of terms. I can find no middle course between love and hatred, cruelty and kindness, truth and falsehood, or any of the great, incontrovertible opposites that is excellent or compatible with enlightened self-interest or the principles of a genuine civilization." "A middle course," Keller concluded, "is really a compromise with evil, it is the same as luke warmness."[4]

One of the most striking characteristics of Keller's speeches is the almost constant conflict between absolutes. Keller often expressed these conflicts by using opposing images such as light versus darkness. She equated light and related metaphors such as day, sun, star, brightness, dawn, and waking up with life, change, power, knowledge, freedom, strength, justice, truth, and hope, while darkness and related metaphors such as night and sleep equaled death, silence, hate, old, despair, ignorance, and stagnation. Her rhetoric contains abundant examples of this. She even titled one of her speeches "A New Light Is Coming." She concluded this speech given in Sagamore Beach, Massachusetts, July 8, 1913, in the following manner:

> But some of us are waking up. We are finding out what is wrong with the world. We are going to make it right. We are learning that we live by each other, and that the life for each other is the only life worth living. A new light is coming to millions who looked for light and found darkness, a life to them who looked for the grave, and were bitter in spirit. We are part of this light. Let us go forth from here shafts of the sun unto shadows. With our hearts let us see, with your hands let us break every chain.

Keller's speech "Onward, Comrades!" New York City, December 31, 1920, included a plethora of light/dark and related metaphors and many of the images she associated with these terms:

> Onward, comrades, all together, onward to meet the dawn. . . .
> March on, O comrades, strong and free, out of darkness, out of silence, out of hate and custom's deadening sway! Onward, comrades, all together, onward to the wind-blown dawn!
> With us shall go the new day, shining behind the dark. With us shall go power, knowledge, justice, truth. . . . There are bright lights ahead of us, leave the shadows behind! In the East a new star is risen! With pain and anguish the old order has given birth to the new, and behold in the East a man-child is born. . . . Onward to the coming dawn!

Through the night of our despair rings the keen call of the new day. All the powers of darkness could not still the shout of joy in faraway Moscow! Meteor-like through the heavens flashed the golden words of light. . . . Words sun-like piercing the dark . . . bidding the teeming world of men to wake and live! Onward, comrades, all together, onward to the bright, re-deeming dawn!

. . . "Halt not, O comrades, yonder glimmers the star of our hope, the red-centered dawn in the East! Halt not, lest you perish ere you reach the land of promise." Onward, comrades, all together, onward to the sun-red dawn!

We march through trackless wilds of hate and death. . . . Over our mur-dered dead we march to the new day. Onward, comrades, all together, on-ward to the spirit's unquenchable dawn!

Keller did not limit her frequent use of light and dark metaphors to her socialist years. For example, the theme of her "Commencement Address to Queen Margaret College," Glasgow, Scotland, June 15, 1932, is that "[t]wo lights are in your horizon for you to choose." Most of this brief speech detailed the two lights in a series of opposites:

One is the fast-fading, will-o'-the-wisp of power and materialism, the other the slowly rising sun of human brotherhood. Two laws stand to-day opposed, each demanding your allegiance. One is the law of death which daily invents new means of combat; this law obliges the nations to be ever at war. The other is the law of peace, of labour, of salvation, which strives to deliver man from the scourges which assail him. One looks only for vio-lent conquest, the other for the relief of suffering humanity. Two ways lie open before you, one leading to a lower and yet lower plane of life, where are heard the weeping of the poor, the cries of little children, and the moans of pain, where manhood and womanhood shrivel, and possessions destroy the possessor; and the other leading to the highlands of the mind where are heard the glad shouts of humanity, and honest effort is re-warded with immortality.

With the dialectical opposition of light and dark, Keller framed a major theme of her discourse—many people were socially and spiritu-ally blind and deaf. In "A New Light Is Coming," she explained what she meant by social blindness and deafness: "It seems to me that they are blind indeed who do not see that there must be something very wrong when the workers—the men and women who produce the wealth of the nation—are ill paid, ill fed, ill clothed, ill housed. Deaf indeed are they who do not hear the desperation in the voice of the people crying out against cruel poverty and social injustice."

The theme of social blindness and deafness presented another con-flict as Keller pitted physical blindness and deafness against the social type, emphatically declaring that the social was worse. Also in "A New Light Is Coming," she claimed, "I have the advantage of a mind trained to think, and that is the difference between myself and most people, not my blindness and their sight." Likewise, when asked on the vaudeville tour, "Which is the greatest human affliction, deafness, dumbness, blindness?" she responded, "None." "Boneheadedness," she exclaimed, was far worse. At still another point, Keller declared, "The facts which they spread before us show that it is not physical blindness, but social blindness which cheats our hands of the right to toil."[5]

Keller stated that a fundamental relationship existed between social blindness and industry. "If I ever contribute to the Socialist movement the book that I sometimes dream of," she remarked, "I know what I shall name it: *Industrial Blindness and Social Deafness*." In explaining how her study of the causes of blindness led her to the workplace, she elaborated on the negative aspects of industry, the dark parts of her dichotomous view of the world. She was forced, she said, to look at "a world of misery and degradation, of blindness, crookedness, and sin, a world struggling against the elements, against the unknown, against itself." She expressed dismay at what she found: "My darkness had been filled with the light of intelligence and, behold, the outer daylit world was stumbling and groping in social blindness!" Keller made frequent pleas to put an end to preventable blindness often caused by poverty and unsafe work conditions. In some speeches she seemed to believe that simply exposing cases of preventable blindness would halt the "blinding ignorance among mankind." In other speeches her view was less naive but no more moderate. She argued cynically that often the sighted were truly blind and the hearing truly deaf to the hum of humanity's voices: "I have walked with people," she declared, "whose eyes are full of light, but who see nothing in wood, sea, or sky, nothing in city streets, nothing in books. What a witless masquerade is this seeing!"[6]

Keller saw the world through her sense of touch, the use of her hand. She frequently discussed the hand in her rhetoric. In fact, she entitled one essay "The Hand of the World." In it she contrasted the big tasks that the hands of laborers do with the little rewards that go into their own hands:

Why is it that so many workers live in unspeakable misery? With their hands they have built great cities, and they cannot be sure of a roof over their heads. With their hands they have opened mines and dragged forth with the strength of their bodies the buried sunshine of dead forests, and they are cold. They have gone down into the bowels of the earth for diamonds and gold, and they haggle for a loaf of bread. With their hands they erect temple and palace, and their habitation is a crowded room in a tenement. They plow and sow and fill our hands with flowers while their own hands are full of husks.

At another point in the essay, Keller associated opposing and conflicting meanings to the image of the hand as she vividly depicted its power to cause good *or* evil:

> Nothing on earth is so thrilling, so terrifying, as the power of our hands to keep us or mar us. All that man does is the hand alive, the hand manifest, creating and destroying, itself the interest of order and demolition. . . . With our hands we raise each other to the heights of knowledge and achievement, and with the same hands we plunge each other into the pit. . . . Misguided hands that destroy their own handiwork and deface the image of God! Wonderful hands that wound and can bind up, that make sore and can heal, suffering all injuries, yet triumphant in measureless enterprise! What on earth is like unto the hands in their possibilities of good and evil? So much creative power has God deputed to us that we can fashion human beings round about with strong sinews and noble limbs, or we can shrivel them up, grind living hearts and living hands in the mills of penury. This power gives me confidence. But because it is often misdirected, my confidence is mingled with discontent.

To Keller, then, the hand represented both the struggle within human beings and the struggle within society. She seemed aware that these struggles were fraught with conflicts: "O pitiful blindness! O folly that men should allow such contradictions—contradictions that violate not only the higher justice, but the plainest common sense."[7]

The conflicting ways that Keller portrayed the hand related to yet another conflict frequently discussed in her rhetoric—socialism versus capitalism. She criticized capitalism for valuing machines over the hands that created them: "The worker has no share in the increased production due to improved methods; and, what is worse, as the eagle was killed by the arrow winged with his own feather, so the hand of the world is wounded by its own skill. The multipotent machine displaces the very hand that created it. The productivity of the machine seems to be valued above the human hand." Keller called the capitalist system a "fraud" and a "mockery of freedom." Again, she used forceful, unequivocal language and framed almost every sentence in antithetical terms. Further examples abound. The following from her speech on the "Menace of the Militarist Program," New York City, December 19, 1915, is typical:

> The only moral virtue of war is that it compels the capitalist system to look itself in the face and admit it is a fraud. . . .

> Why don't you make a junk heap of your master's religion, his civiliza-
> tion, his kings and his customs that tend to reduce a man to a brute and
> God to a monster?

Keller even went so far as to connect capitalists with con artists and suggest they were murderers. For example, in several speeches she made
accusations similar to those in this speech on the "Menace of the Militarist Program":

> In spite of the historical proof of the futility of war, the United States is
> preparing to raise a billion dollars and a million soldiers in preparation for
> war. Behind the active agitators for defense you will find J. P. Morgan & Co.,
> and the capitalists who have invested their money in shrapnel plants, and
> others that turn out implements of murder. They want armaments be-
> cause they beget war, for these capitalists want to develop new markets for
> their hideous traffic.[8]

If Keller portrayed capitalists as all bad, it is no surprise that she
viewed workers as all good. Her antithetical way of thinking may be seen
in the terms she used to label capitalists and workers: She called capitalists "masters," "oppressors," and "enemies," while workers were "slaves,"
"victims," and "comrades." In speech after speech, she used strong, absolutist language, implying that no middle ground existed. The following
examples from two speeches are typical:

> If you doubt that there is any such connection between our prosperity and
> the sorrows of others, consult those bare but illuminating reports of indus-
> trial commissions and labour bureaus. They are less eloquent than ora-
> tory, less pleasant than fiction, but more convincing than either. In them
> you will find the fundamental causes of much blindness and crookedness,
> of shrunken limbs and degraded minds. ("The Conservation of Eyesight")

> I think the workers are the most unselfish of the children of men. . . .
> The workers have no liberties of their own; they are not free when they are
> compelled to work twelve or ten or eight hours a day. They are not free
> when they are ill paid for their exhausting toil. They are not free when their
> children must labor in mines, mills and factories or starve, and when their
> women may be driven by poverty to lives of shame. They are not free when
> they are clubbed and imprisoned because they go on strike for a raise of
> wages and for the elemental justice that is their right as human beings.
> ("Strike Against War")

In this last example, the repetition of "they are not free" added to the
force of Keller's point as did her use of strong words such as "compelled,"
"starve," "driven," "clubbed," and "imprisoned."

Just as workers were all good, so was the socialist system. Socialism, Keller maintained, "goes to the root of *all* poverty and *all* charity" and seeks "the establishment of love and brotherhood and social justice for *every* man and woman upon earth." Socialism equaled a *true* democracy, meaning "equal opportunity for *all*." In a true democracy, "*every* child [would] have a chance to be well born, well fed, well taught and properly started in life," "*every* woman [would have] a voice in the making of the laws under which she lives," and "*all* men [would enjoy] the fruits of their labor" (emphases added).⁹

When Keller's personal metamorphosis changed her from an advocate of peaceful change to a champion of revolutionary reform, she again framed her transformation in contrasting terms. For example, she explained, "This is not a time of gentleness, of timid beginnings that steal into your life with soft apologies and dainty grace. It is a time for loud voiced, open speech and fearless thinking; . . . a time of all that is robust and vehement and bold." She became a member of the Industrial Workers of the World (IWW) because she believed that the Socialist Party was moving too slowly. The IWW, she explained, accepted as a fundamental principle "that there can be no compromise so long as the majority of the working class lives in want while the master class lives in luxury." No compromise seems remarkably similar to her declaration years earlier that "a middle course is really a compromise with evil, it is the same as luke warmness."¹⁰

Keller's rhetoric often contained action steps, and her language in urging these actions was again powerful and absolute. "Up! Up! Something must be done. We have delayed too long," comes from her speech "Our Duties to the Blind," given when she was still an undergraduate. Her later radical rhetoric included even stronger and more urgent action steps, often in the form of antithetical statements. A typical example is the conclusion of her speech "Strike Against War." Here she implored listeners to act unequivocally:

> Strike against all ordinances and laws and institutions that continue the slaughter of peace and the butcheries of war. Strike against war, without you no battles can be fought. Strike against manufacturing shrapnel and gas bombs and other tools of murder. Strike against preparedness that means death and misery to millions of human beings. Be not dumb, obedient slaves in an army of destruction. Be heroes in an army of construction.

In numerous other messages, Keller used similar absolute and antithetical language urging workers to revolt against capitalists in order to win freedom from their enslavement and to organize as a group. She argued that peace could not occur until this happened. She advocated revolution with the same absolute language she had used to advocate more peaceful means of change. For example, in an interview about why she had become a member of the IWW, she was asked, "What are you committed to—education or revolution?" Again, she framed her answer in a contrast: "Revolution. We can't have education without revolution. We have tried peace education for 1,900 years and it has failed. Let us try revolution and see what it will do now."[11]

The constant conflicts that Keller constructed in her rhetoric paralleled the constant conflicts in her life. As I shall show in the next chapter, many people accused Keller of being a "fraud." Her rhetoric recorded her fights against her critics to earn the freedom to speak about a world she could not see. The major conflicts in Keller's discourse paralleled her personal battles to be able to speak her mind freely about all issues that interested her. She fought against physical blindness and deafness just as she advised audiences to fight social and spiritual blindness and deafness. Life had not been just to Keller; she was a victim who depended on others for survival. Similarly, Keller claimed, workers needed to oppose the injustice of poverty, oppression, unsafe work conditions, and the capitalist system in general. Keller gained emancipation from her dark world through thought and language just as, she argued, workers would gain emancipation from the dark world of the capitalist system by making informed choices and by calling for social change. Rhetorical critic Susan Fillippeli summarized how Keller's personal life corresponded to her rhetoric:

> Our analysis revealed that Keller's life was filled with struggle. First she was involved in a struggle to communicate with other humans, and then in a fight to be recognized as a contributing member of society. Keller's rhetoric was structured around the struggle of the workers to be free from the injustice of capitalism. Freedom was the goal that Keller sought in her life as well as in her discourse.[12]

Archetypal Metaphors in Opposition

Most of Keller's metaphors were what rhetorical critic Michael M. Osborn has labeled "archetypal," meaning the associations are timeless, cross-cultural, grounded in experiences common to all human beings, and symbols of fundamental human motivations. The category of archetypal images discussed in most detail by Osborn is light/darkness. As I indicated earlier in this chapter, Keller especially favored light/dark images. In his article "Archetypal Metaphor in Rhetoric: The Light-Dark Family," Osborn explained the significance of a preference for light/dark metaphors:

> Light (and the day) relates to the fundamental struggle for survival and de-
> velopment. Light is a condition for sight, the most essential of man's sen-
> sory attachments to the world about him. With light and sight one is in-
> formed of his environment, can escape its dangers, can take advantage of
> its rewards, and can even exert some influence over its nature. . . .
>
> In utter contrast is darkness (and the night), bringing fear of the un-
> known, discouraging sight, making one ignorant of his environment—vul-
> nerable to its dangers and blind to its rewards. One is reduced to a helpless
> state, no longer able to control the world around him.[13]

It is not surprising that a blind woman would use many light and
dark metaphors, since light and dark are related to sight and survival.
Osborn has explained how frequent use of light and dark metaphors
nourishes and nurtures an elemental, black/white view of the world.
He wrote, "When light and dark images are used together in a speech,
they indicate and perpetuate the simplistic, two-valued, black-white
attitudes which rhetoricians and their audiences seem so often to pre-
fer," and "The situation has been simplified until there are two—and
only two—alternatives, one of which must become the pattern for the
future."[14]

Osborn has also noted an often-neglected aspect of frequent light
and dark combinations: They help enhance the credibility of the speaker
because the images are based on life cycle events that naturally and always occur:

> The combination of light-dark metaphors is ideally suited to symbolize
> such confidence and optimism, because light and dark are more than
> sharply contrasting environmental qualities. They are rooted in a fixed
> chronological process, the movement of day into night and night into day.
> Therefore, symbolic conceptions of the past as dark and the present as
> light or the present as dark and the future as light always carry with them a
> latent element of determinism.[15]

The optimistic tone of Keller's speeches probably contributed to her
effectiveness as a speaker. She helped abled and disabled people believe
they could succeed. She gave hope to people all over the world. It seems
fitting that the name "Helen" comes from the root for "light."

Keller's use of stylistic devices contributed to her effectiveness in part
because she often drew her images from more than one area of experience. For example, she frequently combined light/dark images with images of water and the sea, both archetypal categories according to Osborn and, in fact, the only two archetypal forms that Osborn has written
about separately. Keller's explanation of her life before learning language is typical:

Have you ever been at sea in a dense fog, when it seemed as if a tangible white darkness shut you in, and the great ship, tense and anxious, groped her way toward the shore with plummet and sounding-line, and you waited with beating heart for something to happen? I was like that ship before my education began, only I was without compass or sounding-line, and had no way of knowing how near the harbour was. "Light! give me light!" was the wordless cry of my soul, and the light of love shone on me in that very hour.[16]

Osborn has discussed the rhetorical significance of frequent use of images of water and the sea. In tracing the changes in the meanings of these images, he has written at length about how the technology of the industrial revolution caused writers and speakers with poetic minds to turn to use water and sea imagery to represent freedom, moral beauty, and a sense of renewal. In Osborn's words, "As the day of technology dawned, and workers swarmed into the cities to provide human grist for its machines, the urban experience . . . quite soon seemed intolerable." Osborn quoted dramatic poet W. H. Auden as observing that the Romantics "'saw urban democracy . . . destroying the heroic individual and turning him into a cipher of the crowd, or a mechanical cogwheel in an impersonal machine.'" Both Auden's and Osborn's words seem remarkably similar to the words Keller used in her speeches and writings. For Keller, as for Romantics like Auden, sources of water became refuges, places to escape the oppression of the new urban life. The following statement from Keller's speech "Onward, Comrades!" is typical: "Onward, comrades, all together, onward to the life-giving fountain of dawn!"[17]

Osborn's research has revealed that categories of archetypal metaphors also include the following: family, war/peace, disease/cure, structures, and the sense of space (vertical and horizontal). Keller used each of these types of metaphors extensively and almost always in opposition.

Familial images helped her to express her vision for a better tomorrow. She frequently argued that all people in the world belong to one human family. The following remark is typical:

When indeed shall we learn that we are all related one to the other, that we are all members of one body? Until the spirit of love for our fellowmen, regardless of race, color or creed, shall fill the world, making real in our lives and our deeds the actuality of brotherhood—until the great mass of the people shall be filled with the sense of responsibility for each other's welfare, social justice can never be attained.[18]

Similarly, in the last line of her speech "A New Light Is Coming," Keller said, "We shall be 'just one great family of friends and brothers.'"

Given that Keller was a pacifist, it is not surprising that many of her speeches treated the topic of war and that her rhetoric contained many images dealing with war and peace. Again, examples abound, including the following taken from her "Address to the National Council of Women": "I believe women can make the world safe from war, and it is incumbent upon them to use this power before it is too late." The next statement is interesting because it supports the importance she accorded to rhetoric: "We must learn to think down every wall that divides us from our fellow-creatures and prevents us from giving them sympathy and help." According to Keller, thinking and communicating would help achieve peace. She concluded the speech, "Whole-heartedly I join hands with all who, like the National Council of Women, go forth to liberate, to enlighten and to bless. Always in my dreams I hear the turn of the key that shall close for ever the brazen gates of war, and the fall of the last rampart that stands between humanity and a happier world."

Given that blindness and deafness are diseases, it is not surprising that Keller often chose disease and cure metaphors. Her "Address to the Rotarians of Inverness," Scotland, September 8, 1932, provides a typical example:

> It would be wonderful if the Rotarians should exert their united influence to keep the light in the eyes of unnumbered millions of people throughout the British Empire. We live in a redemptive world. Earth has no hopeless islands or continents. My friends, will you not inscribe upon your banner: "Health is the Natural State of Man. Poverty, the root of disease, will end."

Generally, Keller advanced her arguments on both moral and practical grounds. In her speech "Our Duties to the Blind," she reasoned aloud about how it made economic sense to give able-bodied blind people the opportunity to work; her explanation typified her use of structural images in speeches: "To teach Latin and Greek and higher mathematics to blind pupils, and not to teach them to earn their bread, is to build a house entirely of stucco, without stones to the walls or rafters to the roof."

A group of images that Osborn did not mention but that certainly fits his definition of archetypal is the land. Keller's images often concerned the land—nature, earth, climate, trees, flowers, harvest, and so forth. The conclusion of her speech "Onward, Comrades!" contained several, as she talked about the young men who had died in war:

> The valiant young men of all lands eagerly seeking life's great enterprises, love, adventure and the fair country of bright dreams. Under our feet they lie, mingling their clean young flesh with the soil, the rain and the heat!

Over our murdered dead we march to the new day. Onward, comrades, all together, onward to the spirit's unquenchable dawn!

In a letter to neurologist Dr. Frederick Tilney, Keller explained how her sense of smell helped her sense the scents of types of wood, fruits, and seeds. In discussing smelling a campfire from a great distance, she wrote, "This makes me feel a kinship to the Indians; for I, also, can smell at a great distance."[19]

Given the importance of the hand to Keller's ability to survive in the world, it is not surprising that she often discussed it and tried to prove that it was a universal image. Consider the import Keller accorded the hand in the following statement: The number of words formed from the Latin root for hand, *manus*, was enough "to name all the essential affairs of life." "All life," she continued, "is divided between what lies on one hand and on the other." The hand, she claimed, "has conquered the wilderness. The laborer himself is called a hand. In *man*acle and *man*umission we read the story of human slavery and freedom." The hand, then, Keller argued, was a timeless, cross-cultural image common to all people; to her it served as an archetypal image that, like other images, she used in contrast.

Although Keller clearly presented the world as a place of opposing tensions and conflicts, she expressed optimism that good would triumph over evil. She even wrote a book of essays entitled *Optimism*. She concluded almost every speech in a positive tone, frequently ending with one or more archetypal images. Below is the ending of *each* of the orations in the "Collected Speeches" section of this book; these speeches span time, place, and subject matter:

I hope you will all come to South Boston some day and see what the little blind children do, and then go out to the beautiful child's garden and see little Tommy and pretty Willie, the little girl from Texas. ("Speech at Andover")

Sometime, somewhere, somehow we shall find that which we seek. We shall speak, yes, and sing, too, as God intended we should speak and sing. ("Address of Helen Keller at Mt. Airy")

Surely Massachusetts will not now turn a deaf ear to the cry of the helpless adult blind. . . . Therefore I have complete faith in the ultimate triumph of our cause. ("Our Duties to the Blind")

I appeal to you, give the blind man the assistance that shall secure for him complete or partial independence. He is blind and falters. Therefore go a little more than half-way to meet him. Remember, however brave and self-reliant he is, he will always need a guiding hand in his. ("The Heaviest Burden of the Blind")

Let our battlecry be, "No preventable disease, no unnecessary poverty, no blinding ignorance among mankind." ("The Conservation of Eyesight")

Let us here and now resolve that every deaf child shall have a chance to speak, and that every man shall have a fair opportunity to make the best of himself. Then shall we mend the broken lyre of human speech and lessen the deafness and blindness of the world. ("The Gift of Speech")

Let us go forth from here shafts of the sun unto shadows. With our hearts let us see, with your hands let us break every chain. Then, indeed, shall we know a better and nobler humanity. For there will be no more slaves. Men will not go on strike for 50 cents more a week. Little children will not have to starve or work in mill and factory. Motherhood will no longer be a sorrow. We shall be "just one great family of friends and brothers." ("A New Light Is Coming")

Why don't you make a junk heap of your masters' religion, his civilization, his kings and his customs that tend to reduce a man to a brute and God to a monster? Let there go forth a clarion call for liberty. Let the workers form one great world-wide union, and let there be a globe-encircling revolt to gain for the workers true liberty and happiness. ("Menace of the Militarist Program")

Be not dumb, obedient slaves in an army of destruction. Be heroes in an army of construction. ("Strike Against War")

Onward, comrades, all together, onward to the spirit's unquenchable dawn! ("Onward, Comrades!")

I appeal to you, Lions, you who have your sight, your hearing, you who are strong and brave and kind. Will you not constitute yourselves Knights of the Blind in this crusade against darkness? ("Speech to Annual Convention of Lions Clubs International")

When I consider how the deaf and the blind are led out of the house of bondage by the work of their teachers, I realize what shall some day happen to mankind when the highest education is attained. ("Address to the Teachers of the Deaf and of the Blind")

Your life is stretched between the least that is left behind and the achievement still before you, of which every vision that we get seems only a glimmer of the truth that we shall some day win. Like your patron saint you will go forth to civilize, to enlighten, and to bless. Yes, you are going toward something great. I am on the way with you, and therefore I love you. ("Commencement Address to Queen Margaret College")

Yes, the teachings of Emanuel Swedenborg have been my light and a staff in my hand, and by his vision splendid I am attended on my way. ("Address to the New Church of Scotland")

A daily walk in the sweet fields of the Word renews our faded enthusiasms and enlarges our aspirations. We have not learned the Lesson of Life if we do not every day open the Word for a moment of spiritual refreshment. ("Address in St. Bride's Parish Church")

If people everywhere would only minimize their differences and think of the fine qualities that unite them, they would strive to bring order and unity out of the discords created by fear and strife. True patriotism now is to unite in casting our weight on the side of all work that liberates, enlightens, and turns disaster into a bridge-road to a nobler civilization. ("Address to the National Institute for the Blind")

Whole-heartedly I join hands with all who, like the National Council of Women, go forth to liberate, to enlighten and to bless. Always in my dreams I hear the turn of the key that shall close for ever the brazen gates of war, and the fall of the last rampart that stands between humanity and a happier world. ("Address to the National Council of Women")

Certainly, dear Lions, it would gratify me inexpressibly if through your bounty the blind of all Latin America might draw freely from the waters of literature to satisfy their cravings of the mind and the spirit. ("Speech to Knights of the Blind")

Keller's widespread use of archetypal images in dialectical opposition is a distinct characteristic of her rhetoric. We may wonder why a person lacking the two most basic senses would make such frequent use of imagery in contrast. Her Western classical literary education provides one possible reason. She was thoroughly grounded in the works of the great thinkers of Western thought. Western culture values absolutist language, linear thinking, either-or patterns of organization, choosing between alternatives, people as controllers of their environment, and speakers as agents of change. These values promote a dichotomous orientation to the world where people perceive life as consisting of tensions between fundamental oppositions and conflicts. The tensions and conflicts contribute to the speeches' success because they touch a human cord that is central to this culture.

The creation story, as told in Genesis, gives insights into the dichotomous way of thinking characteristic of Western culture and found in Keller's speeches. The story consists of a poetic narrative about archetypal images, usually in opposition. On the first day, God created *light* and *dark* and *contrasted* the two. On the second day, He *divided* the *sky above* from the *waters below*. Day three involved dry *land versus water, continents versus oceans*. The words *earth* and *nature* appear frequently here. The first mention of *day versus night* occurs on day four as God created the sun, moon, and stars. Day five followed from day two: God created *birds* (in the sky *above*) and *fish* (in the sea *below*). On the sixth day, God created all other *animals,* including *people* whom He created in His image. The emphases are added here to demonstrate how the primal, archetypal images of the biblical creation story correspond remarkably to the images used by Keller in her rhetoric. Even many of the divisions correspond, such as light *versus* dark and day *versus* night. Stories of creation give insights into cultures by reflecting how the cultures perceive themselves.

For Keller, creation took on added significance. She viewed creation and speech as intrinsically interrelated, crediting speech with transforming her from merely *existing* to really *living.*

In Western society generally, students learn to speak and write by imitation, the assumption being that studying great speakers and writers will help students become great speakers and writers. Although Keller read many works, she could read only those works that had been translated into Braille. These consisted almost exclusively of works by Western writers. Thus, it is not surprising that she imitated qualities characteristic of Western civilization.

Besides learning to speak and write, children learn about the world in general by being told by elders what they can and cannot do. Several studies have found that American children hear the word *no* in their early years more frequently than any other word. This conclusion must apply even more to a deaf-blind person whose world is more dangerous than the world of most children. Learning language within the context of *thou shalt not* and *thou shalt* also may have contributed to Keller's fondness for metaphors in contrast.

As evidence that other methods for teaching children exist, consider this idea explained by a Native American woman in discussing Cherokee teachings:

> When children argued about an object, it was removed and the children were encouraged to observe the sky. Elders reminded the children that placing attention on an object and seeking to possess it takes one outside the circle of harmony. The children were then invited to relate the vast completeness of their experience with the vastness of the sky. "Look at the clouds. What do you see? Can you see the sky beings?" Thus attention was placed on openness so large that no one had any desire to possess it.[20]

Another possible reason for Keller's frequent use of archetypal images in opposition is that she learned by association. For example, she understood the word *red* because Teacher had explained that a burning fire was red. The necessity to learn and understand by association meant that Keller had to live and think in images reflecting the constructed binary ideology that permeates Western civilization.

Keller's use of contrasting metaphors may also have been affected by how the press treated her. Newspapers generally described young Helen as a "witch." As soon as she learned language, newspapers suddenly referred to her as an "angel."

No matter what the cause, Keller's extensive use of images in contrast characterized her rhetoric and reflected the Western culture that shaped her. Since Western thought divides, segments, and categorizes experiences, Keller used archetypal metaphors in a way that likewise divided, segmented, and categorized experiences, resulting in messages that reflected a binary way of thinking and that were fraught with oppositions and tensions.

The extensive use of sensory images and rare use of intellectual images were other important characteristics of Keller's speeches. *Sensory images* refer to words and phrases that evoke images that listeners can see, hear, smell, taste, or feel; *intellectual images* refer to all images that are not sensory. According to rhetorical critic Carroll C. Arnold, "Sensory images tend to stimulate listeners to experience vicariously; to that extent the linguistic form invites them to become experientially, hence feelingly, involved in what is said." Keller's figurative forms included images dealing with blindness and deafness and sight and sound. Generally, she chose images that were broad, sweeping, timeless, and inclusive rather than narrow, folksy, or specific to particular situations or audiences. Keller's wide use of figures of speech sometimes brought abstract and complex ideas into the immediate ken of varying audiences. They helped Keller identify with her audiences. In short, they added to the persuasive and poignant power of her speeches.[21]

In general, forms of figuration are difficult to refute because they appeal to the imagination. Keller's reliance on sensory images, forms of figuration that by definition encouraged listeners "to experience vicariously," made them even more difficult to refute. In her speech "Strike Against War," she refuted "fear advanced as argument for armament" by telling a fable:

A certain man found a horseshoe. His neighbor began to weep and wail because, as he justly pointed out, the man who found the horseshoe might someday find a horse. Having found the shoe, he might shoe him. The neighbor's child might some day go so near the horse's heels as to be kicked, and die. Undoubtedly the two families would quarrel and fight, and several valuable lives would be lost through the finding of the horseshoe. You know the last war we had we quite accidentally picked up some islands in the Pacific Ocean which may some day be the cause of a quarrel between ourselves and Japan. I'd rather drop those islands right now and forget about them than go to war to keep them. Wouldn't you?

In this passage, Keller invited listeners to participate in her reasoning, and she included at least the following categories of archetypal forms: family, war, and a sense of space. To refute her argument, listeners needed to criticize themselves and/or not identify with images common to all human beings.

Keller invited audience participation also by frequent use of rhetorical questions, questions where the answers are implicit. By definition, these questions involved listeners, encouraging them to think of their own answers and seeing if their answers matched Keller's. "Wouldn't you?" a question asked in "Strike Against War," is an example of a rhetorical question. Of course, listeners, who for this speech consisted almost exclusively of workers and union representatives sympathetic to her cause, answered to themselves, "Yes, I would." In her speech "Menace of the Militarist Program," Keller asked a series of rhetorical questions to prove that this country is a "mockery of freedom":

> What have you to fight for? National independence? That means the masters' independence. The laws that send you to jail when you demand better living conditions? The flag? Does it wave over a country where you are free and have a home, or does it rather symbolize a country that meets you with clenched fists when you strike for better wages and shorter hours? Will you fight for your masters' religion which teaches you to obey them even when they tell you to kill one another?

Sometimes Keller directly invited listeners to participate. For example, in her speech "Onward, Comrades!" she twice implored her listeners to "halt not," and once asked her listeners to "pause one panting moment and shed a tear for the youth of the world, killed in its strength and beauty—our brothers, our comrades, tenderly loved." In her "Address to the Rotarians of Inverness," she involved the audience more extensively:

> Will you try a little experiment? Then, close your eyes tightly, so that you cannot see a ray of light. This room, the faces of your friends—where are they? Everything you have seen daily vanishes, the street, the sky, and the stars. Remember, with you this catastrophe is make-believe. You can at will open your eyes and see again, while the child born blind, or the man blinded by accident or disease, must live in the dark as long as life lasts.[22]

Keller's tendency to involve her audiences helped her to identify with them. She also identified with listeners by broadening issues so as to include as many people as possible. Even when she spoke to raise consciousness and collect money for the blind and deaf, she generally broadened the topic, treating abled as well as disabled people. For example, in "The Gift of Speech," she moved from discussing the needs of the deaf to the needs of all humankind, as can be seen in the following sentence: "Let us here and now resolve that every deaf child shall have a chance to speak, and that every man shall have a fair opportunity to make the best of himself." Keller was concerned with the interests not just of blind and deaf people but of all people. Her speeches concerned a vision of a better tomorrow for all human beings. She seemed to feel a special responsibility to affect future life on earth. In "Strike Against War," she said, "The future of the world rests in the hands of America." The speech concerned the special responsibility of Americans to help make the world's future more fair, decent, loving, and caring.

Keller's frequent references to the Bible and use of religious language also helped her to identify with audiences. She was thoroughly familiar with the Bible. As a young adult, she wrote about the importance of the Bible in her life:

> I began to read the Bible long before I could understand it. Now it seems strange to me that there should have been a time when my spirit was deaf to its wondrous harmonies. . . . But how shall I speak of the glories I have since discovered in the Bible? For years I have read it with an ever-broadening sense of joy and inspiration; and I love it as I love no other book.

Keller's thoughts and feelings about the Bible persisted throughout her life. As an older woman, even after writing a book on the Swedenborgian religion, she gave an entire speech on how the Bible served as a source of hope, courage, joy, and balance. In "Address in St. Bride's Parish Church," she said the Bible had always been a "blessing" to her.[23]

Other archetypal images identified by Osborn and used by Keller occur frequently also in the Bible. These include: family, war and peace, and disease and cure. In addition, many terms often appear both in the Bible and in Keller's speeches, including the following: *dawn, change, life, freedom, sleep, death, silence, hate, ignorance, blind, deaf, dumb, speak, see, hear, power, truth, knowledge, masters, oppressors, bondage, fetters, rejoice, blessing, finger, touch, love, angel, chorus, chains, shadow, open, key, perish, brought forth, deliver, jewel, holy, freedom, spirit, eternal,* and *Word.* While many of these words are common, other expressions used by Keller are not typical of everyday speech, but they, too, come from the Bible. Examples include "the dews of Hermon," the "Lamb of God," and the "Garden of

Eden." In short, Keller infused almost every speech with religious words and images.

The religious tenor of Keller's speeches may have been the product of how she was treated by the press. Reporters repeatedly referred to her as an example of the potential of the human spirit to triumph over adversity. To many, she was—and still is—a lesson in courage. Keller's audiences, then, probably expected her speeches to contain a moral lesson. Using biblical language and a religious tone may have been ways Keller purposefully adapted to her audiences.

Keller frequently combined religious language and archetypal images. The following remark from her "Address to the National Institute for the Blind" is typical:

> I stand before you, myself deaf and blind, and with halting speech I plead with you to do unto my blind fellows as you would have others do unto you. Remember, blind people are just like other people in the dark. They have the same ambitions and feelings you have. They want the same things you do. They want work, useful work and some of life's sweet satisfactions. When the public adopts an attitude of understanding and helpfulness, the difficulties of the sightless will no longer be insurmountable. Through you they will triumph over blindness. Only then will God's Commandment be obeyed, "Put not a stumbling-block in the way of the blind, nor make life bitter for the deaf."

In addition to the biblical tradition, Keller borrowed from Greek mythology, Romantic poetry, Marxist rhetoric, and mysticism. In general, her images were derivative; they were not startling, new images but, rather, the images used in the upbeat rhetoric of hope, new beginnings, and a Union with God. In general, Keller's language was lofty and poetic, and it incorporated ideas and images from several traditions popular at the time. Interweaving several different traditions was another way that Keller identified with audiences: Listeners who did not identify with one set of images could identify with another. For example, the following passage from her speech "Address to the Teachers of the Deaf and of the Blind" uses imagery from several traditions:

> And what shall I say of the skill and devotion of those who open doors of opportunity for the sightless! When teachers awaken the dormant faculties of a deaf or blind pupil, Prometheus-like they must steal the fire of heaven, and with it put life into what is inert and light up a darkness that has no end. Generations rise up and call themselves blessed because they have lighted the lamp of thought in many minds.

In short, Keller's speeches made wide use of various forms of figuration. Her figures of speech were piquant, pungent, pithy primitive, and picturesque. They infused her speeches with life, adding vivacity to the ideas, so they were difficult for listeners to forget. Use of various forms of figuration helped Keller state her points precisely. Her poetic, poignant, penetrating, and powerful speeches helped her to identify with her audiences.

Keller's audiences varied. Especially between 1915 and 1960, she often found herself "On the Road Again," speaking in lecture halls and parlors across the United States and the world. She spoke with the Chautauqua lecture circuit, took part in a vaudeville tour, and made a silent movie entitled *Deliverance.* In 1924, she became the chief spokesperson for the American Foundation for the Blind. When Teacher died in 1936, Polly Thomson accompanied Keller. During World War II, Keller spoke to the wounded in hospitals, always offering messages of hope. On behalf of the American Foundation for the Blind, she traveled the world, raising money for the blind, advocating for their needs and for the needs of all people, and serving in general as a charitable humanitarian.

Keller's fame catapulted her into worldwide prominence as an altruistic American heroine. Her popularity and people's curiosity to see and hear a deaf-blind person probably added to the large numbers in Keller's audiences. Numerous newspaper reports of speeches discuss these crowded audiences; often, all available seats were taken, and hundreds of people were turned away.

The pattern for Keller's typical lecture consisted first of Teacher describing "the miracle" of Helen learning language. Then Teacher helped Keller onto the platform where Keller demonstrated her lipreading skills and answered questions from the audience. Then Keller delivered her speech, usually broadening the difficulties of blind and deaf people to the difficulties of workers and average people.

Reports of Keller's delivery describe her voice as disagreeable—harsh, monotonous, and lacking modulation and vocal variety. But she generally spoke slowly, so listeners could understand most of her words, and she usually appeared alert. Her radiant face, gentle disposition, expressive body movements, and stylish clothes helped to make her speeches successful.

Summary and Conclusions

Today most people know of Helen Keller as the bright, spunky girl at the end of the film, *The Miracle Worker.* Keller was a bright, spunky girl, but she was also much more. She was a pacifist, a suffragist, a socialist, and a member of the IWW. She held unorthodox views throughout her lifetime.

Most Keller scholars either ignore these nontraditional stances or minimize them by attributing them to her concern that poverty causes certain types of blindness, and she was committed to eradicating blindness. Keller's reformist ideas, however, went deep into her core. They were manifestations of her view of the world as a constant conflict between absolutes, especially between good and evil. Her rhetoric records the struggles she saw, such as light versus darkness and the hand as a metaphor for oppression versus the hand as a metaphor for constructive change. Keller's broad humanitarian interests and her deep concern for the rights of workers relate to her view of the world as a place with no middle ground.

Keller's rhetoric inspires, but it also includes cynicism and sarcasm. She was an angelic and animated speaker, but she also was an activist, a reformer, and a fiery orator. We can learn more from her rhetoric by demystifying her and hearing what she really had to say.

3

Just Because I Cannot See
Doesn't Mean I Cannot Know

*My teacher is so near to me that I scarcely think of myself apart from her.
How much of my delight in all beautiful things is innate, and how much is
due to her influence, I can never tell. I feel that her being is inseparable from
my own, and that the footsteps of my life are in hers.*

— *Helen Keller,* The Story of My Life

In the above passage, Helen Keller noted how her life was linked inextricably to the life of her Teacher, Anne Sullivan. This interconnectedness became Keller's blessing and curse. As Sullivan's biographer Nella Braddy Henney wrote in the "Introduction" to Keller's book *Teacher,* "As long as Annie Sullivan lived . . . a question remained as to how much of what was called Helen Keller was in reality Annie Sullivan."[1]

Throughout Keller's life, some people raised this question about her rhetoric, claiming that she could not have written most of her speeches, books, and articles because she had not experienced the things she spoke and wrote about; they especially questioned her frequent use of visual and auditory imagery. Teacher, the doubters claimed, wrote Keller's messages for her. These indictments of Keller's rhetoric were especially frequent during the period when she actively advocated such political causes as socialism and pacifism. Keller responded adamantly to the accusations that she had not written her messages, defending her right to think, speak, and write independently and about issues not directly concerned with blindness and deafness. In this chapter, I shall examine the charges leveled against Keller and her retorts. I shall focus also on how certain aspects of both the criticisms and replies parallel certain ideas on the nature of language.

Helen Keller Is a "Dupe of Words"

To support their claims that Helen Keller could not possibly have written the words she spoke and wrote, critics usually employed one or more of

Keller smelling a rose. She insisted that her senses of smell and touch equipped her to understand the world.

OLD SERIES, VOL. 46
NEW SERIES, VOL. 10 | No. 49.   BOSTON, SATURDAY, DECEMBER 5, 1896.   PER ANNUM, $2.50.
SINGLE COPIES, 5 CENTS

Keller on the cover of Boston's *Home Journal*, 1896. From the time she was a young girl through her adulthood, people showed interest in this "miraculous" person who found light in darkness and song in silence.

the following techniques: (1) They argued that she could not possibly know about things she could not experience; (2) they showed that her senses of touch, smell, and taste did not compensate for her loss of sight and hearing; (3) they dismissed her as only a "girl"; (4) they considered her a victim used by others to further selfish and sinister agendas; (5) they referred to an incident in her childhood where she plagiarized; or (6) they referred to ideas about language acquisition.

Throughout her life Keller frequently faced critics who argued that she did not possess the ability to understand the world she lived in; without the two most important faculties, these critics maintained, she was incapable of knowing about anything dealing with sight and sound. Because she could not possibly know about such things, the ideas in her speeches and writings could not represent her own thoughts; they had to represent the thoughts of sighted/hearing people. For example, critics claimed that Keller could not have understood the color "red" since she had never seen anything red. A review in the New York *Nation* (and reprinted in the *New York Post*) of Keller's first autobiography, *The Story of My Life*, explained the reasoning of this argument: "All her knowledge is hearsay knowledge, her very sensations are for the most part vicarious, and yet she writes of things beyond her powers of perception with the assurance of one who has verified every word." The reviewer concluded that if Keller "were to be judged like less afflicted mortals, we should have to call a great deal of Miss Keller's autobiography 'unconscientious'" because it lacked "literary veracity" and was an example of "literary insincerity." Another reviewer asserted that Keller could not possibly know about issues involved in everyday life: "Talking is to her a newly discovered art," so she speaks "of things concerning which she knows nothing, *could not possibly know anything*" (emphasis added).[2]

Both in Keller's lifetime and today, a prevailing stereotype about blind and deaf people is that their superior senses of touch, smell, and taste compensate for their missing sense(s). Scientists, neurologists, psychologists, physiologists, educators, and others subjected Keller to numerous experiments and tests. Continually, the results showed that in general the three primary senses Keller possessed—touch, smell, and taste—were not superior to those of seeing/hearing people. So, critics contended, Keller lacked the two most important faculties, and her other faculties did not compensate for this loss.[3]

Critics also pointed to obvious facts: Keller's lack of sight and hearing made her imperfectly equipped to handle everyday tasks without help from Sullivan or others, and she depended on Sullivan for help in speaking and writing. This dependence on Teacher contributed to the belief by some that Keller was incapable of thinking for herself. Rhetorical critic Susan E. Fillippeli explained the reasoning behind this contention: "Since

Keller could not walk unassisted in the world she could not possibly think unassisted about the world." Certainly many people accepted this argument, especially when Keller espoused politically radical views. According to an editorial in the *Common Cause*, an antisocialist publication, "'For twenty-five years Miss Keller's teacher and constant companion has been Mrs. John Macy'" (Anne Sullivan's married name). "'Both Mr. and Mrs. Macy,'" the editorial continued, "'are enthusiastic Marxist propagandists, and it is scarcely surprising that Miss Keller, depending upon this lifelong friend for her most intimate knowledge of life, should have imbibed such opinions.'" Critics frequently blamed Teacher for using a blind, deaf, and mute child to further her personal motives. Sullivan's teaching methods were unorthodox, especially for the time, and many people charged that she used her pupil to advance her selfish educational agenda.[4]

The perception of Keller as victim remained with her throughout her life. As I discussed in the last chapter, Keller spoke and wrote on several controversial topics, including socialism and communism. Generally, when she advocated such causes, instead of blaming her, critics blamed proponents of socialism and communism for taking advantage of a deaf, blind, and mute girl. The two newspaper comments below are typical:

> It would be difficult to imagine anything more pathetic than the present exploitation of poor Helen Keller by the Socialists of Schenectady.

> Is it not rather a pity that one for whom our system of education has done so much as it has for Miss Keller . . . should be induced to write as she does? The pity of it is that it does not reflect upon Miss Keller, but upon those responsible for her education, and for the contact she has had with persons who bear the taint of Communism. . . . We have known of Communists occasionally in the schools and colleges, but did not know that they sought out those without complete physical equipment for the purposes of deception.[5]

Critics frequently tried to minimize Keller's impact on audiences by characterizing her with such labels as "this unfortunate girl" and "poor little Helen Keller." Throughout more than half her life, some people referred to her as a helpless little girl. At a time when women fought to have a voice and a vote in government, women's views on issues carried little weight, making the views of a helpless little girl even easier to dismiss. Fillippeli noted that critics discredited Keller's opinions by calling them those of just a "mere girl" until she was well into her fifties![6]

In *The Story of My Life*, Keller detailed an incident that occurred when she really was a girl. Her public presentation of this event provided support for critics who claimed that she was incapable of thinking, speaking, and writing for herself. When Keller was ten years old, she wrote a story entitled "The Frost King" for Michael Anagnos, director of the Perkins School for the Blind. The story contained several sensory images about the beauty and splendor of fall foliage and about how King Frost painted the trees to "comfort us for the flight of summer." Shortly after Anagnos received the story, it was discovered that words, sentences, paragraphs, and ideas in "The Frost King" paralleled those in Margaret T. Canby's story "The Frost Fairies." No one questioned the similarities, but many people questioned whether Sullivan and/or Keller had knowingly plagiarized the composition and then lied to cover up the dishonesty. Keller and Sullivan insisted that they were unfamiliar with Canby's story; according to the duo, Sullivan had never read the story to Keller. After investigating the matter, Sullivan learned that a friend with whom Keller stayed almost three years earlier when Sullivan was away had read the story to Helen. Keller and Sullivan claimed that Helen's photographic memory allowed her to remember the story's words and ideas years later. Evidence indicting Keller included a report by a teacher at Perkins that recounted a conversation where Keller first admitted that Teacher had read the story to her and afterwards said confusedly, "'Teacher says I must not get mixed up.'" Keller then said that another woman had read Canby's story to her. Another argument used against Keller was the inability of any person to remember entire passages verbatim three years after hearing them read just one time.[7]

A tribunal concluded that the case was "not proven": Testimony failed to prove that Keller or Sullivan willfully deceived; neither did testimony exonerate the pair by proving the veracity of their account of the episode. Joseph Lash, author of the definitive biography on Keller, claimed that Sullivan and Keller had lied. Teacher, he asserted, had read the Canby story to her pupil several times. Lash posited the possibility that Sullivan did not know the meaning of *plagiarism* prior to this incident, and he argued, like many others before and after him, that Keller would have said whatever her Teacher asked her to say.

Of course, we will never know for sure what really happened in "The Frost King" incident. However, this event has several important implications. First, it underscored the extent to which Helen, the child, had already catapulted to national prominence. Most ten-year-olds in similar situations would be chastised in private, not investigated in public. The episode also represented an early example of Keller being cast as a victim. Most people who did not believe Keller's explanation of the incident blamed not her but Sullivan. Teacher, these critics charged, had taught Keller to cheat, lie, and generally deceive. After the incident, Anagnos called Keller a "living lie" but added that she was not to blame; the fault lay with Sullivan for teaching this innocent girl to lie. Perceiving Keller as a victim in "The Frost King" situation was not limited to friends and acquaintances, as the following comment reveals: "The *Goodson Gazette* does not blame little Helen Keller for the attempt at fraud, far from it. She is not to blame. She has merely done what she was told to do. The blame for fraud rests not upon her, but upon whoever knowingly attempted to palm off the Frost King as her composition and there the blame will lie." This accusation is directed, of course, at Sullivan, who critics consistently portrayed as a selfish, stubborn, and headstrong woman.[8]

A final way that critics attacked Keller's ability to compose the words she spoke and wrote was by referring to theories of language. Many empiricist philosophers of the time maintained that words are representations for objects that people can understand *only* if they perceive the objects directly. Anagnos's predecessor Samuel Gridley Howe accepted and advocated this conception of language. He stated the core of the argument succinctly: "Strictly speaking, words are objects" because "words are substitutes for the thing." Howe taught his pupil Laura Bridgman, the first blind, deaf, and mute individual to receive a systematic education, to attach names to objects. All people, of course, begin to acquire language by this type of labeling, but Bridgman never moved beyond this point in her linguistic development. She never used visual or auditory imagery probably because her teacher Howe believed that the blind "can never understand certain words or phrases because they have never experienced the sensations which they are intended to express."[9]

The ideas of phrenologist George Combe influenced Howe. According to Combe and other phrenologists, certain mental faculties were indicated by the configuration of a person's skull. One of these faculties was language. The language faculty controlled the capability of inventing and understanding signs including words, but, significantly, this faculty was "cognizant of *signs alone*, the *meaning* of which is acquired by the other faculties." Thus, faculties other than the language faculty understood color, form, size, and so forth. Because meanings of words depended on direct sensory perceptions of objects that these words represented, blind people could never comprehend the meanings of words involving color, form, or size. Combe offered this explanation: "A blind man, by the aid of the faculty of Language, may learn to connect his own notions of a horse with the name: but his conceptions will be very different from those attached to it by a person who sees; for the blind man could not judge of its colour at all, and not very correctly of its form and size."[10]

Literary critic Mary Krag Klages explained how people who embraced this "materialistic philosophy of language" naturally would accept Keller's use of words involving sight and sound as a form of plagiarism:

One could thus "own" words, as one "owned" objects or things, if one could establish possession of the meaning of words through direct sensory experience of the objects they represented. Keller, lacking the two most important senses, could not "own" words descriptive of sight and sound; when she employed them, she committed a form of theft, stealing their meanings from others' experiences.[11]

In his book *The Blind in School and Society,* psychologist Thomas D. Cutsforth, himself blind after age eleven, launched a massive attack on Keller's speaking and writing and on Sullivan's method of educating her charge. According to Cutsforth, blindness was not just the lack of sight; rather, "blindness changes and utterly reorganizes the entire mental life of the individual." Like Howe and Combe, Cutsforth argued that words are symbols for sensory perceptions. Educators like Anne Sullivan who taught the blind in the same way as sighted people ignored reality; they were teaching "the seeing who could not see" to use words representing perceptions that blind people could not possibly perceive. According to Cutsforth, Keller's descriptions were merely "pretenses at enjoying and appreciating that which she does not experience," and her writing was really "implied chicanery" because she "sacrificed reality on the altar of literary hypocrisy." Professor Pierre Villey, himself also blind, was a strong defender of Keller, but nonetheless he reached a similar conclusion: He called Keller "a dupe of words," explaining that "her aesthetic enjoyment of most of the arts is a matter of auto-suggestion rather than perception."[12]

Significantly, like others before and after him, Cutsforth did not blame Keller but rather blamed Sullivan: "The implied chicanery in this unfortunate situation," he wrote, "does not reflect upon the writer personally, but rather upon her teacher and the aims of the educational system in which she has been confined during her whole life." According to Cutsforth, Keller was unable to "discriminate between the real and the unreal" because she lived "in a world which does not exist." Keller, however, had no choice, continued Cutsforth, because her Teacher placed a higher value on literary education than on other aspects of education and because in attempting to make Keller as much like sighted and hearing people as possible, Sullivan had ignored the unique experiences of this extraordinary blind and deaf child. Lash concurred with Cutsforth's assessment:

> Cutsforth's criticism of Teacher's methods had merit. Helen's education, because of Teacher's own limitations as well as Helen's handicaps . . . had been excessively literary. Given Helen's mental powers, it is interesting to speculate whether she might not have made reports from the world of

darkness of even greater help to scientist, philosopher, and educator, and to the deaf-blind if she had had a teacher who, like William James, stressed the importance of thinking *things*, not words.[13]

In sum, throughout her life and especially after "The Frost King" incident, doubters, skeptics, and cynics questioned the ability of an imperfectly equipped person to understand the whole of life. To most critics Keller was a fairytale princess victimized by socialists, communists, and especially her Teacher. The criticisms levied against Keller lessened her credibility with some listeners, and the frequency and intensity of the attacks forced her to develop several rhetorical strategies for defending her right to have a legitimate voice.

Helen Keller Responds

Throughout her life and especially during her socialist years, Keller needed to respond to the criticisms leveled against her. In speech after speech, she used one or more of the following rhetorical strategies to defend her right to speak: (1) focusing on similarities to sighted/hearing people, especially on her ability to think, read, and obtain information; (2) asking critics to fight fairly; (3) giving doubters the burden of proof; (4) emphasizing that she lived in the same world and used the same language as sighted and hearing people; (5) insisting that the senses she possessed were sufficient for understanding the world; (6) using analogies and associations; and (7) highlighting the supremacy of the soul and of the spiritual sphere.

Focusing on Similarities to Sighted/Hearing People

In her rhetoric Keller repeatedly minimized differences and stressed similarities between herself and people who could see and hear. She especially emphasized her ability to think and to read. In *Midstream,* she quoted Descartes's famous maxim "I think, therefore I am" and claimed that this truism "worked something in me that has never slept since." That we do not think with our eyes and ears is obvious, but Keller repeatedly stated this obvious fact in defending her right to speak. As early as 1904, Keller devoted the beginning of speeches to defending this right. For example, in "Our Duties to the Blind," she said: "I have heard that some people think the views I am expressing on this subject, and indeed on all subjects, are not my own, but Miss Sullivan's." Keller continued by citing her Teacher's credentials in considerable detail, indicating that she used her as a resource just as she used other "wise sources." She ended her defense of her right to speak by saying, "But may I venture to protest I have some ideas of my own?"[14]

In "A New Light Is Coming," Keller spent over one third of the speech justifying why she had the right to express her views:

> Ever since I came here, people have been asking my friends how I can have a first-hand knowledge of the subjects you are discussing. They seem to think that one deaf and blind cannot know about the world of people, of ideas, of facts. Well, I plead guilty to the charge that I am deaf and blind, though I forget the fact most of the time. It is true, I cannot hear my neighbors discussing the questions of the day. But, judging from what is repeated to me of their discussions, I feel that I do not miss much. I can read.

To bolster her credibility, Keller frequently explained her reading habits in considerable detail. She often named specific authors as she did in "A New Light Is Coming": "I can read the views of well-informed thinkers like Alfred Russell Wallace, Sir Oliver Lodge, Ruskin, H. G. Wells, Bernard Shaw, Karl Kautsky, Darwin and Karl Marx." Sometimes she pointed to her ability to read in several languages, including English, French, German, Greek, and Latin. Often she spoke about places she had visited such as factories, slums, and shops; her sources of information, she argued, were just as reliable as those of sighted/hearing people.

Primarily, Keller underscored the fact that she obtained information about local, national, and world issues and events the same way all people obtain their information—through thinking, reading, discussing, and debating. All people, she claimed, gain the majority of their knowledge through mediated communication in the form of words. They learn by conversing with others; by reading books, magazines, and newspapers; and by listening to radio and ultimately television. In speech after speech, she stressed that she learned about issues and events in this same way. The majority of what all people read and hear, she said, represents "the accumulated experience of our ancestors and contemporaries as it is handed down and given over to us in words." In "A New Light Is Coming," she explained these points in detail:

> Of course, I am not always on the spot when things happen, nor are you. I did not witness the dreadful accident at Stamford the other day, nor did you, nor did most people in the United States. But that did not prevent me, any more than it prevented you, from knowing about it.
>
> To be sure, I have never been a captain of industry, or a soldier, or a strikebreaker. But I have studied these professions, and I think I understand their relation to society. At all events, I claim my right to discuss them. I have the advantage of a mind trained to think, and that is the difference between myself and most people, not my blindness and their sight.

By focusing on her ability to think, read (even works in other languages), and obtain information in the same way as all people, Keller shifted the audience's attention from her disabilities to her abilities.[15]

Keller repeatedly expressed frustration and anger at people who wanted her to speak and write only about herself. Other people, she exclaimed, were not confined to speaking and writing *only* about their direct experiences. Why, then, should she be? In the preface to *The World I Live In*, she elaborated:

> Every book is in a sense autobiographical. But while other self-recording creatures are permitted at least to seem to change the subject, apparently nobody cares what I think of the tariff, the conservation of our natural resources, or . . . reform of the educational system. . . . But until they give me the opportunity to write about matters that are not-me, the world must go on uninstructed and unreformed, and I can only do my best with the one small subject upon which I am allowed to discourse.

Keller criticized people who claimed that the deaf-blind "have no moral right to talk about beauty, the skies, mountains, the song of birds, and colors." To Keller, the critics' argument equaled saying, "I may not talk about beautiful mansions and gardens because I am poor. I may not read about Paris and the West Indies because I cannot visit them in their territorial reality. I may not dream of heaven because it is possible that I may never go there."[16]

Asking Critics to Fight Fairly

At times Keller's frustration took the form of sarcasm and ridicule. She insisted that focusing only on how she differed from sighted/hearing people was not fair fighting and urged critics not to pity *her* but to challenge her *ideas*. The opening of her speech "Strike Against War" typifies her frequent pleas for critics to fight fairly:

> To begin with, I have a word to say to my good friends, the editors, and others who are moved to pity me. Some people are grieved because they imagine I am in the hands of unscrupulous persons who lead me astray and persuade me to espouse unpopular causes and make me the mouthpiece of their propaganda. Now, let it be understood once and for all that I do not want their pity; I would not change places with one of them. I know what I am talking about. . . . All I ask, gentleman, is a fair field and no favor.

In a letter to Senator Robert M. La Follette supporting his bid for the presidency, Keller stated succinctly her desire for a fair fight: "Opposition does not discomfort me when it is open and honest. I do not mind having my ideas attacked and my aims opposed and ridiculed, but it is not fair fighting or good argument to find that 'Helen Keller's mistakes spring out of the limitations of her development.'"[17]

When Keller wrote about "mistakes spring[ing] out of the limitations of her development," she may have been referring to an article published twelve years earlier that she quoted in her essay "How I Became a Socialist":

> The Brooklyn *Eagle* says, apropos of me, and Socialism, that Helen Keller's "mistakes spring out of the manifest limitations of her development." Some years ago I met a gentleman who was introduced to me as Mr. Mc-Kelway, editor of the Brooklyn *Eagle*. . . . At that time the compliments he paid me were so generous that I blush to remember them. But now that I have come out for Socialism he reminds me and the public that I am blind and deaf and especially liable to error. I must have shrunk in intelligence during the years since I met him. . . . The *Eagle* and I are at war. . . . When it fights back, let it fight fair. Let it attack my ideas and oppose the aims and arguments of Socialism.[18]

Giving Doubters the Burden of Proof

Throughout her life, Keller expressed extreme frustration at people who refused to see beyond her physical handicaps. In addition to asking critics to fight fairly, she maintained that those who raised doubts about her capabilities possessed the burden of proof. In other words, Keller argued, critics needed to prove that she was inherently different from sighted and hearing people. Although she often proved that she was similar to people who could see and hear, she claimed that she did not have the responsibility of proving this. In her words, "Some brave doubters have gone so far even as to deny my existence. In order, therefore, that I may know that I exist, I resort to Descartes's method: 'I think, therefore I am.' Thus I am metaphysically established, and I throw upon the doubters the burden of proving my nonexistence."[19]

Posing questions was a technique used by Keller to give critics the burden of proof. She frequently ended a discussion defending her right to speak and write about things she could not physically see or hear by asking one or more rhetorical questions, questions where the correct answers are implicit. Below are typical examples:

> Has anything arisen to disprove the adequacy of correspondence? Has any chamber of the blind man's brain been opened and found empty? Has any psychologist explored the mind of the sightless and been able to say, "There is no sensation here?"

When we consider how little has been found out about the mind, is it not amazing that anyone should presume to define what one can know or cannot know?[20]

Discussing Her World and Language

In addition to stressing how *she* was like sighted and hearing people, Keller argued that she lived in the same *world* and used the same *language* as sighted and hearing people. Although she could not see or hear, she lived in a five-sensed world and learned a language full of words referring to the senses. No special vocabulary existed for the blind and deaf. If such a vocabulary did exist, Keller could communicate only with other blind and deaf people, and people who could see and hear would not be able to understand her. But such was not the case. Whether or not people agreed with Keller, they could understand her. This occurred, she said, because she inherited the same world and the same language as all people. In *The World I Live In*, she gave the following explanation:

> The blind child—the deaf-blind child—has inherited the mind of seeing and hearing ancestors—a mind measured to five senses. Therefore he must be influenced, even if it be unknown to himself, by the light, color, and song which have been transmitted through the language he is taught, for the chambers of the mind are ready to receive that language. The brain of the race is so permeated with color that it dyes even the speech of the blind. . . . If the dark silent world which surrounds him were essentially different from the sunlit, resonant world, it would be incomprehensible to his kind, and could never be discussed. . . . If the mental consciousness of the deaf-blind person were absolutely dissimilar to that of his fellows, he would have no means of imagining what they think.

Keller further underscored the fact that she *had* to use the same language as all people with an analogy comparing the deaf-blind child to a sailor on an island where everyone spoke an unfamiliar language. The sailor, she said, "must learn to see with their eyes, to hear with their ears, to think their thoughts." Why, Keller asked, should she not say "I see" and "I hear" when these are what she thought?[21]

Keller further insisted that her tendency to think as if she had all five senses was involuntary and habitual. She had read and "heard" so much about sights and sounds that they naturally became part of her language and, hence, of her discourse. To clarify, she offered the following analogy: "When a man loses a leg, his brain persists in impelling him to use what he has not and yet feels to be there. Can it be that the brain is so constituted that it will continue the activity which animates the sight and the hearing after the eye and the ear have been destroyed?"[22]

Keller did not claim that her understanding of color, sculpture, music, and so forth, was *exactly* the same as that of people with all their faculties; she contended only that there was *sufficient* similarity between her world and the world of others since she could live in both worlds simultaneously and be understood in both. "Perhaps my sun shines not as yours," she said. "The colors that glorify my world . . . may not correspond exactly with those you delight in; but they are none the less color to me. The sun does not shine for my physical eyes, . . . nor do the trees turn green in the spring; but they have not therefore ceased to exist, any more than the landscape is annihilated when you turn your back on it."[23]

The way Sullivan chose to teach language to her pupil contributed to Keller's adamant conviction that her world was fundamentally similar to the world of all people. As I discussed in Chapter 1, Sullivan taught Helen just as she would teach a sighted and hearing child. She talked into her pupil's hands almost constantly. Her descriptions included numerous references to colors, shapes, sounds, and other things that many people argued depended on the ability to see and hear to understand.

Before "The Frost King" episode, Keller's education in language and literature consisted largely of imitating writers she admired and incorporating their words, diction, style, tone, and ideas into her own writing. Keller put it this way:

> This habit of assimilating what pleased me and giving it out again as my own appears in much of my early correspondence and my first attempts at writing. . . . Those early compositions were mental gymnastics. I was learning, as all young and inexperienced persons learn, by assimilation and imitation, to put ideas into words. Everything I found in books that pleased me I retained in my memory, conscientiously or unconsciously, and adapted it.

In the same discussion, Keller referred to a composition she wrote at age eleven that she read at the graduation ceremony of the Perkins School: "Italy is a country rich in beauty, beautiful blue skies, lovely scenery; rich, too, in works of art,—grand cathedrals, beautiful paintings and statues; rich, also, in poetry and music. Oh, Italy! land of song and of flowers! How happy I shall be when I am old enough to visit her great cities, for books and friends' descriptions have made them dear to me!"

Keller assumed Anagnos realized that an eleven-year-old child could not have originated the ideas in this piece; she had to have borrowed and assimilated these ideas. Before "The Frost King" incident, Anagnos and others had complimented Keller for her ability to borrow and assimilate aspects of other people's writings and conversations. This, of course, changed after the plagiarism case, making Keller afraid to speak or write because she could not always distinguish her words and ideas from the words and ideas she read or had spelled into her hands.[24]

Of course, all people face the difficulty of not knowing if their ideas are original or an assimilation of what they have read or heard. The problem for Keller, however, was more acute because more of her reality was mediated. Generally people receive more information through books, magazines, newspapers, conversations with others, and so forth, than through direct experiences. Keller's direct experiences, however, were more limited than those of "normal" people. Hence, her reliance on mediated sources of communication was more frequent. Her reality was essentially a linguistic reality because so many of her experiences came to her through the eyes and ears of other people.

John Albert Macy, the husband for a short time of Sullivan and the editor of Keller's *The Story of My Life,* contended that critics should commend rather than condemn Keller for trying to speak and write like seeing and hearing people:

> [If Keller] had not tried to be like other people, if her teacher had not made her try, we should never have heard of her. . . . Only by trying to be what other people are, by trying to do what they do, by trying to use a language she has never heard, by learning of things she has never seen and trying to grasp them as completely as she could, and write and speak about them as fully and as often as she could, only by striving to forget and deny her limitations, has she realized herself and given the lie to her afflictions.

Macy argued that Keller should be praised for imitating others, for she "herself was mute, and her imitation is a splendid woman with speech."[25]

Stressing the Adequacy of Her Senses

Keller defended her frequent use of images involving touch, smell, and taste by demonstrating the degree of detail she digested without the distractions of sights and sounds. She spoke about how she could detect doctors, painters, sculptors, masons, carpenters, ironworkers, druggists, artists, and cooks just from their odors. She explained that southern towns smelled of cornbread, yams, fried chicken, and grits, while northern towns smelled of corned beef, doughnuts, fishballs, and baked beans. She spoke about her ability to distinguish between Protestant and Catholic churches, business and residential areas, and city and country roads. The following exemplify the degree of detail typical of Keller's descriptions:

Fifth Avenue, for example, has a different odour from any other part of New York or elsewhere. . . . I recognize expensive perfumes, powders, creams, choice flowers, and pleasant exhalations from the houses. In the residential section I smell delicate food, silken draperies, and rich tapestries. Sometimes, when a door opens as I pass, I know what kind of cosmetics the occupants of the house use. I know if there is an open fire, if they burn wood or soft coal, if they roast their coffee, if they use candles, if the house has been shut up for a long time, if it has been painted or newly decorated, and if the cleaners are at work in it.

Hold out your hands to feel the luxury of the sunbeams. Press the soft blossoms against your cheek, and finger their graces of form, their delicate mutability of shape, their pliancy and freshness. Expose your face to the aerial floods that sweep the heavens, "inhale great draughts of space," wonder, wonder at the wind's unwearied activity. Pile note on note the infinite music that flows increasingly to your soul from the tactual sonorities of a thousand branches and tumbling waters.[26]

Keller insisted that the senses she possessed, especially touch, were adequate for understanding the world. She stated emphatically that the impressions she gathered through touch were real and alive to her, even if others claimed they were unreal and lifeless. Her senses functioned as the alchemy by which with three senses she could communicate with people who possessed five senses. Her fingers were like ten eyes and ten ears, sensitive to the sights and sounds around her. They constituted her reality.

Keller argued that sense of touch was *more* important than visual or auditory senses: "I am sure," she exclaimed, "that if a fairy bade me choose between the sense of sight and that of touch, I would not part with the warm, endearing contact of human hands or the wealth of form, the mobility and fullness that press into my palms." Keller sometimes used the authority of another person to support her claim about the importance of touch: "In my classification of the senses, . . . touch is a great deal the eye's superior. I find that great artists and philosophers agree with me in this. Diderot says: "'I found that of the senses, the eye is the most superficial, the ear the most arrogant, smell the most voluptuous, taste the most superstitious and fickle, touch the most profound and the most philosophical.'"[27]

Keller's defense of her sense of touch makes sense given that, as I showed in the last chapter, the hand served as an important symbol in her rhetoric. Keller called the hand "the symbol of the race." Her many discourses about the hand include the following statements:

Look in your *Century Dictionary* . . . and learn how many idioms are made on the idea of the hand, and how many words are formed from the Latin root manus—enough words to name all the essential affairs of life.

All our earthly well-being hangs upon the living hand of the world. Society is founded upon it.

On the hand of the world are visible the records of biology, of history, of all human existence.

The hand of the world . . . now obscurely symbolizes—the uplifting and regeneration of the race, all that is highest, all that is creative in man.

By characterizing the hand as at the root of "enough words to name all the essential affairs of life," as the foundation of society, as a record "of all human existence," and as the hope for the "uplifting and regeneration of the race," Keller tried to prove that her sense of touch enabled her to understand the world in which she lived. The frequent use of absolute language when talking about the hand (such as "all" in the three examples above and "highest" in the last instance) further maximized the importance of the hand. Personifying the hand and sometimes using the adjective *living* before *hand* were other ways that Keller showed that her sense of touch gave her adequate knowledge of the world around her. Finally, Keller frequently used religious language when discussing the hand. The following statement combined personification and religious language: "The eye cannot say to the hand, 'I have no need of thee.' Blessed be the hand!"[28]

Keller responded to critics who pointed to the numerous tests showing that her senses of touch, smell, and taste were not superior to everyone else's by distinguishing between capability and use. She argued that her senses were especially acute and discriminating because necessity required her to train and cultivate more of their potential ability. She dealt with the experimental findings also by discussing the finite nature of the senses compared to the infinite nature of the mind. After personally expecting to learn of the superiority of her sensory abilities but instead learning of their normality, Keller commented, "Ruefully you try to save face by explaining to your inquisitors that your impressions of the world do not come through the senses alone, but through the magical medium of imagination and association of ideas which enter your mind as detached, chaotic physical experience, and are synchronized into harmonious entity which is your conception of the universe."[29]

In addition to stressing the adequacy of her senses, Keller stressed the adequacy of her mind. She admitted that the problems of the blind are enormous, but blindness, she exclaimed, does not affect a person's mind. Keller discussed a period in her life when she temporarily lost her sense of smell. Even without her olfactory sense, she remarked, she could think clearly. She articulated the enthymematic chain of her reasoning. "My temporary loss of smell proved to me, too, that the absence of a sense need not dull the mental faculties and does not distort one's view of the world, and so I reason that blindness and deafness need not pervert the inner order of the intellect." The use that people make of their minds was to Keller what separated the blind and deaf from the sighted and hearing: "We differ, blind and seeing, one from another, not in our senses, but in the use we make of them, in the imagination and courage with which we seek wisdom beyond our senses." People's physical senses, of course, can be limited; ignorance can likewise limit the mind. Limitations may occur in any configuration: People may have all five senses and a good mind, one or more impaired senses and a good mind, all five senses and a poor mind, or one or more impaired senses and a poor mind. Keller always spoke of herself as someone with two impaired senses but a superb mind.[30]

Using Analogies and Associations

The power of association, according to Keller, was what allowed her, like all people, to relate things she could not experience to things she could experience. Through association and analogies, she understood words she could not know through direct sensation. The analogies often involved the three primary senses she possessed—touch, smell, and taste. She frequently interwove all five senses, linking odor to sight, touch to sound, and so forth. For example, she explained, "I understand how scarlet can differ from crimson because I know that the smell of an orange is not the smell of a grape-fruit" and "The hardness of the rock is to the hardness of wood what a man's deep bass is to a woman's voice when it is low."[31]

The use of analogies may have come easily to Keller because Teacher often employed detailed and complex analogies when describing people, places, events, and things. One example will suffice:

> My teacher read me "The Chambered Nautilus," and showed me that the shell-building process of the mollusks is symbolical of the development of the mind. Just as the wonder-working mantle of the Nautilus changes the material it absorbs from the water and makes it a part of itself, so the bits of knowledge one gathers undergo a similar change and become pearls of thought.[32]

Keller argued that she was not unique in using association and analogy. She contended that all language is learned through these processes. For example, all people understand abstract words by employing analogies, relating the known to the unknown: "All people attach certain meanings to abstract terms" that "cannot be represented truly by visible objects, but which are understood from analogies between immaterial concepts and the ideas they awaken of external things."[33]

Keller's argument that all language is learned through association and analogy is similar to the argument made by some rhetorical and literary scholars who claim that all language is metaphorical. For example, in his *Philosophy of Rhetoric*, I. A. Richards criticized the limited, traditional view that treated metaphor as an added power of style. Traditional theorists, he contended, "think the image fills in the meaning of the word; it is rather the other way around and it is the word which brings in the meaning which the image and its original perception lack." In contrast to the traditional view, Richards posited that "thought is metaphoric" and that "metaphor is the omnipresent principle of language." Like Keller, Richards argued that language itself develops by associations between the known and the unknown, the familiar and the unfamiliar.[34]

I cannot overemphasize the importance Keller accorded the abilities of association and analogic reasoning to relate what she knew through direct experience to what she inferred about things she could not experience. She frequently spoke about analogies and associations, and she often used these words in her discourse. She also frequently talked about "similarities," "correspondences," "resemblances," and "likenesses." The following statement is not something Keller actually said, but the spirit of the statement epitomizes her response to critics who claimed she "stole" language by using words descriptive of color and sound: "When I say it's hot as hell, it doesn't mean I've been there!"

Highlighting the Supremacy of the Soul

The primary way that Keller minimized her differences from other people and stressed her similarities was by highlighting the power and supremacy of the soul. People's physical senses could be limited, but the soul was limitless. All people's sense experiences, claimed Keller, were laden with shortcomings, imperfections, deceptions, fallibilities, and limitations. Whether people possessed three or five senses made little difference. The presence of these imperfections bridged the chasm between deaf/blind and the sighted/hearing world. Keller remarked that discovering and accepting the imperfection of people's physical senses helped her to feel "as one who had been restored to equality with others, glad, not because the senses avail them so little, but because in God's eternal world, mind and spirit avail so much." Through the soul, Keller could "see" and "hear" all things because her soul possessed perfect senses. Because her soul, spirit, and faith possessed inner eyes and ears that could see and hear perfectly, she declared that she could use words descriptive of sights and sounds.[35]

Like language, Keller claimed, the soul served as her liberator. It provided her refuge from dark days and silent nights. It emancipated her from the isolation caused by the deep, total, enveloping darkness and silence that constituted her world. It helped her to overcome feelings of inadequacy, insecurity, and helplessness; she could feel comforted and confident by the assurance that she was still in this world, still connected to people and things around her. For Keller, the soul confirmed her existence. As she put it, "To everyone with faith his own world is real, no matter what it may appear to be to others."[36]

Understanding the spiritual world came easily to Keller. As she put it, "To one who is deaf and blind, the spiritual world offers no difficulty. Nearly everything in the natural world is as vague, as remote from my senses as spiritual things seem to the minds of most people. . . . The inner, or 'mystic' sense, if you like, gives me the vision of the unseen."[37]

Although this inner vision came easily to Keller, she argued that all people possessed a "soul sense" or what she also called a "sixth sense": "Each individual has a subconscious memory of the green earth and murmuring waters, and blindness and deafness cannot rob him of this gift from past generations. This inherited capacity is a sort of sixth sense—a soul sense which sees, hears, feels, all in one."[38]

Keller's discussions of the supremacy of the soul were broad based. She argued that "the bulk of the world's knowledge" was "an imaginary construction." She gave several examples: "History is but a mode of imagining, of making us see civilizations that no longer appear upon the earth," philosophers "can never perceive the world in its entirety," poets and musicians "cease to use the crude instruments of sight and hearing," astronomers cannot see all the intricacies of the planets and stars. Even developments in science, the most empirical of fields, "owe their origin to the imagination of men who had neither accurate knowledge nor exact instruments to demonstrate their beliefs."[39]

Keller's convictions about the soul related to her emerging religious views. In her book *My Religion,* she described a startling experience where "a sudden flash of intuition revealed an infinite wonder to me." While reading about Greece, she suddenly felt transported there and, in fact, shouted, "'I have been in Athens.'" She explained what then occurred: "Scarcely were the words out of my mouth when a bright, amazing realization seemed to catch my mind and set it ablaze. I perceived the realness of my soul and its sheer independence of all conditions of place and body. It was clear to me that it was because I was a spirit that I had so vividly 'seen' and felt a place thousands of miles away." The experience demonstrated to Keller that her infirmities "were of no real account." The "uncircumscribed Spirit" was all that mattered.[40]

The theological works of Emanuel Swedenborg helped Keller to understand her transformation. In *My Religion,* Keller quoted Swedenborg's recounting of a blind woman who "never doubted that there was a spiritual body within the material one with perfect senses" and whose soul and spirit were "the eyes within her eyes." Keller embraced Swedenborg's convictions and used his ideas in her rhetoric to explain the supremacy of inner vision over actual eyes and of the soul and spiritual sphere over the human body.[41]

Swedenborg had considerable influence on American Transcendentalists of the mid-nineteenth century. For example, he influenced Ralph Waldo Emerson and others of his group; Emerson quoted him. While living in New England during this time, Keller could easily see Swedenborg as a spiritualizing philosopher.

Keller's belief in the supremacy of the soul found support also in the beliefs of several of the philosophers she studied in her philosophy class at Radcliffe. The course was taught by Josiah Royce, a pupil of William James and a famed, monistic, idealist philosopher of the time. He was engaged in pushing philosophy at Harvard/Radcliffe away from C. S. Peirce's pragmatism and from what he viewed as a growing behaviorism in psychology and philosophy. Royce was trying to evolve an idealistic rhetoric, and although he did not seem to have the intent, his ideas and outlook eventually came to inform the idea of communication as inquiry.[42]

Royce's course introduced Keller to major thinkers, including Plato, Bishop George Berkeley, Immanuel Kant, and Ernst Cassirer, whose ideas conformed to the idealistic drift in some of the late nineteenth- and early twentieth-century philosophy in America. Like Keller, many of the philosophers she studied shared her ideas about the relationship between language and objects and about the centrality of the human spirit. Like Keller, these philosophers she studied believed that words are symbols of perceptions, not signs of material objects; that physical senses are imperfect; that meaning comes from the soul, not from direct sensory experiences; and that the human spirit transcends the physical body. Keller discussed this endorsement of her beliefs by philosophers: "Ancient philosophy offers an argument which still seems valid. There is in the blind as in the seeing an Absolute which gives truth to what we know to be true . . . light to what is invisible, music to the musical that silence dulls." About Plato Keller remarked, "I had a joyous certainty that deafness and blindness were not an essential part of my existence, since they were not in any way a part of my immortal mind." Berkeley, an Anglican archbishop, argued that to exist is either to be perceived or to perceive. He denied the existence of matter, claiming there were only perceptions. Kant, founder of "critical" or "transcendental idealism," declared that the objects of sense experiences are merely "appearances." The ideas of all these philosophers and others Keller studied in this and other classes provided her with ammunition to continue her lifelong battle to have the right to think and speak independently. In her words, "Philosophy is the history of a deaf-blind person writ large. From the talks of Socrates up through Plato, Berkeley, and Kant, philosophy records the efforts of human intelligence to be free of the clogging material world and to fly forth into a universe of pure idea." She continued, "Philosophy gives to the mind the prerogative of seeing truth, and bears us into a realm where I, who am blind, am not different from you who see."[43]

In short, Keller's major philosophical growth occurred during a time of philosophical turmoil in the United States. Part of her battle appeared to be with the pragmatism and behaviorism that were growing in American intellectual and social life. Instead, she chose idealism, a position that fit with her socialist stance and with her overriding concerns about humanity. The religious and philosophical ideas of others affirmed and reaffirmed for Keller her own views and served as her *elixir vitae*.

Suggestions for Future Research

Helen Keller, like Laura Bridgman before her, was born a normal, healthy child. She could see. She could hear. She could speak. She lost these faculties at nineteen months of age. Thus, before Keller became blind and deaf, she knew *through direct sensory experience* the relationship between words and things, the meaning of color, and the sound of music. Dr. James Kerr Love is the only scholar I have encountered who focused on this important nineteen-month period. Love raised important questions: "'What had become of the impressions gathered into Helen's mind, and stored away somewhere during the nineteen months of seeing and hearing? Were they lost or had they merely for the time lost their labels?'" Love concluded that Teacher recovered in her pupil "'the once vivid impressions of early childhood—those of colour and sound. Those impressions for a time lost their names, but the percepts were not lost.'" Keller herself hinted at the same conclusion. "In my dreams," she wrote, "I have sensations, odors, tastes, and ideas which I do not remember to have had in reality. Perhaps they are glimpses which my mind catches through the veil of sleep of my earliest babyhood." Another time Keller remarked that "during the first nineteen months of my life I had caught glimpses of broad, green fields, a luminous sky, trees and flowers which the darkness that followed could not wholly blot out.

If we have once seen, 'the day is ours, and what the day has shown.'" Are the conclusions of Love and Keller correct? To what extent and in what ways would Keller's use of language, her conception of words dealing with sight and sound, and her understanding of the world she lived in have been different if she had been born blind and deaf or if she had lost her sight and hearing in more advanced years when her linguistic abilities would have been more developed? I leave these questions to future researchers.[44]

A related question concerns the word *water*. When Keller first learned language as a healthy toddler, her first word was "water" (originally pronounced "wah-wah"). In writing about her young childhood, she noted, "Even after my illness I remembered one of the words I had learned in these early months. It was the word 'water,' and I continued to make some sound for that word after all other speech was lost. I ceased making the sound 'wah-wah' only when I learned to spell the word." When Keller learned language eight years later as a blind and deaf child, her first word again was *water*. Is this simply a striking coincidence, or does the parallel here suggest something about those first nineteen months of life and about the way people acquire language? Again, I hope future researchers will pursue these questions.[45]

Effects and Conclusions

Keller's personal battle to speak her mind freely about all issues that interested her paralleled a frequent theme of her rhetoric—the battle of all human beings to improve their conditions. As discussed in the last chapter, in many speeches and essays, especially during her socialist years, Keller declared that workers needed to revolt against capitalists and industrialists to win freedom from their enslavement. Throughout her life, Keller fought to win the freedom to think, speak, and write independently just as workers fought capitalists to win the freedom to enjoy the fruits of their labor. Keller's conflicts, then, extended beyond her immediate critics. Her lifelong battles included her personal rights, the rights of blind and deaf people, and the rights of all humanity. In "The Gift of Speech," she claimed, "Speech is the birthright of every child." In this chapter, we learned that not only was speech itself a child's birthright but so, too, was the right to speak. As Keller eloquently stated in the peroration to "The Gift of Speech," "Let us here and now resolve that every deaf child shall have a chance to speak, and that every man shall have a fair opportunity to make the best of himself. Then shall we mend the broken lyre of human speech and lessen the darkness and blindness of the world."[46]

To what extent did Keller succeed in proving that she was an intelligent woman capable of understanding the world in which she lived? The answer is complex. On the one hand, several people constrained Keller's freedom. At several points in his book, Lash discussed how Sullivan kept Keller dependent on her. For example, Teacher and Keller's mother prevented Helen, then a thirty-six-year-old woman, from getting married, an indication, wrote Lash, of the extent to which Keller was "a prisoner," unable to follow her dreams and aspirations. For the last half of her life, Keller maintained strong political and social views but ceased actively advocating them in order not to jeopardize the work of the American Foundation for the Blind (AFB). In fact, trustees of the AFB controlled Keller's life to a great extent for many years and in many ways. For instance, before she died in 1968 at age eighty-seven, Keller requested that a Swedenborgian minister be present at her funeral. AFB trustees and Keller's family ignored her wishes. As Fillippeli succinctly stated, "Even in death Keller was not free."[47]

A more subtle constraint on Keller's acceptance as a credible speaker and writer stems from the public's perception of her. Most people know of Keller only as the intelligent, spunky child in the play *The Miracle Worker*. As I shall discuss further in the next chapter, most people who have spoken and written about Keller focus exclusively on how she is a symbol of the triumph of a pure soul over an imperfect body. As I demonstrated in this chapter, Keller was not without critics. But what is unusual about her story is that she remains an angelic, fairytale princess despite the criticisms because almost all critics blame not her but Sullivan and occasionally others for the qualities they criticize. Keller is cast as a "poor little *girl*" and a "*victim*." This twist is particularly intriguing when applied to rhetoric. Critics claimed that Keller did not write her oral and written messages and contended that Teacher was at fault for allowing Keller to present these messages as her own. The critics' argument here is like admonishing a speaker for using a ghostwriter but saying that the ghostwriter is at fault while the speaker is a victim who remains innocent! This twist served as another way of denying Keller's personhood and intelligence.

In other ways, Keller succeeded in proving she was an intelligent, capable, and knowledgeable woman. In an age when the political views of a woman were generally not taken seriously, Keller was literally and figuratively heard by many people. In this way, she contributed to the right of a woman to speak and write about issues outside of the home. Likewise, she strengthened the right of the disabled to speak and write about issues not directly connected to their disability. Critics who tried to silence the silent had met their match in Keller, who seemed to view criticisms as challenges and attempts to silence her as additional reasons to speak. I contend that the arguments Keller advanced to defend her right to speak in a primarily masculine, able-bodied culture were among her most interesting arguments. As long as people continue to read her messages or messages about her, these ideas live on. The popularity of Keller's works attests to her success in proving that she was an intelligent woman capable of thinking, speaking, and writing to improve conditions for all human beings.

4

Not a Muted Voice:
The Effectiveness of Keller's Speaking

The sum of it all is that you are a blessing, and I'll kill anyone who says you are not.

—*William James*

History has accepted James's conclusion and labeled Keller a blessing. Biographers and others have called her "archpriestess of the sightless," "wonder woman," "a modern miracle," and "the eighth wonder of the world." Certainly Keller is a consummate example of someone who "transmuted loss to gain," tragedy to triumph. This chapter details some of the many tangible and intangible effects of her speaking.[1]

Tangible Effects

Many of Keller's speeches were results oriented. She frequently asked audiences to *do* things such as give money. She became, in her words, "an international beggar." Helen began these humanitarian appeals while only a child. For example, as discussed in Chapter 2, instead of replacing her dog who had recently died, Helen engaged in a speech and letter-writing campaign asking people to send money so a blind and deaf boy could have a teacher like hers: "And now I want to tell you what the dog lovers in America are going to do. They are going to send me some money for a poor little deaf and dumb and blind child." This first fund-raising campaign was a clear success. Helen raised over $1,600, enough to support the boy for over two years. As an adult, Keller raised hundreds of thousands of dollars each year.

Another striking example of the success of Keller's speaking occurred in her "Speech to Annual Convention of Lions Clubs International" in 1925. She challenged the Lions to become "Knights of the Blind":

The opportunity I bring to you, Lions, is this: To foster and sponsor the work of the American Foundation for the Blind. Will you not help me hasten the day when there shall be no preventable blindness; no little deaf children untaught; no blind man or woman unaided? I appeal to you, Lions, you who have your sight, your hearing, you who are strong and brave and kind. Will you not constitute yourselves Knights of the Blind in this crusade against darkness?

Lions Clubs International accepted Keller's challenge and established a SightFirst program aimed at four critical areas: health care infrastructure, training of eye care professionals, treatment of blindness and visual impairment, and public education. The SightFirst program has succeeded beyond the organizers' dreams. In the 1993–94 year, for example, the Lions raised $130 million dollars for this major service activity. In addition, the clubs cosponsored a recycling program with approximately 460 LensCrafters stores, offered about 600,000 professional glaucoma screenings for free, and made approximately 25,000 corneal transplants possible. Lions Clubs International also established and supported most of the world's eye banks as well as hundreds of hospitals, clinics, and eye research centers. The organization has provided eye examinations, eyeglasses, Braille-writers, large-print books, canes, guide dogs, and restorative surgery to thousands of people worldwide at no cost.[2]

Keller's speeches and writings directly helped the blind and deaf in a myriad of ways, including the creation of numerous funds and schools for blind and deaf people. Keller always argued that blind and deaf people could, and should, work like able-bodied people and live independent, normal lives. To this end, she helped institute several social reforms, including persuading employers to hire blind and deaf people. Keller also fought for changes in the workplace, such as assembly-line techniques especially suited to blind people and Braille-writers that made jobs for blind people easier to obtain. During World War II, she argued that blind people could help fill the void in labor. Further, she persuaded the Work Progress Administration to establish talking books for the blind. Because of her rhetoric, records could be mailed to anyone postage free. Although she did not like her name used to raise money or promote projects, she allowed it when she believed in the cause. She served as a spokesperson for the rights of the blind and deaf specifically and for humanitarian causes generally.

Keller's success was not limited to the United States. She helped establish schools and funds for the blind and deaf in many countries. In India, for example, she established a national fund and nine schools. In Holland, she participated in the opening of a school to teach deaf children to speak by cultivating their sensitivities to sound vibrations.

Much of Keller's speaking was highly personal. She spoke to thousands of wounded people in military hospitals, bringing hope and inspiration. She advocated blind bowling, golf, and water skiing, Braille recipes, and numerous other items to allow blind and deaf people to live normal lives.

Keller's speeches and writings portray a woman who yearned to make the world a better place. Misery and oppression provoked and riled her to *do* things to better human conditions. She felt the world's woes, deplored them, and spoke out strongly against them. She clearly possessed a vision of a better tomorrow, and her entire being was stirred to fight for this vision. Her rhetoric records the ways she attempted to influence people to accept her ideas, intuitions, and insights.

Almost all of Keller's speeches were successful, in part, because she usually spoke to friendly crowds who shared her views. Most of her inflammatory socialist speeches, for example, were presented to people who already possessed socialist leanings. Hence, although these speeches appear deliberative, trying to convert people's beliefs, they were really epideictic or ceremonial, trying to inspire people to act on their views and values.

Intangible Effects

Perhaps the single factor that contributed most to the success of Keller's speeches was herself. She embodied courage, hope, strength, and valor. Even before she opened her mouth, she was considered successful. Her very presence conveyed a message of strength and inner power; she herself functioned as proof. Here was a miracle people could literally see and hear. A living symbol. An epideictic person. How could audiences not be moved by someone who could find light in darkness and song in silence?

Added to Keller's presence were her compassion, sympathy, and breadth of knowledge. Here was someone who focused on humanity's suffering, not her own. Her themes, words, and manner embodied the simplicity of the truth, the generosity of the spirit, and the purity of the human soul. Her sightless eyes saw, her soundless ears heard, and her strange voice spoke directly to the heart. She touched the lives of millions. She was not a muted voice, but rather, a beloved speaker.

Conclusions

By considering Keller a blessing, a consummate example of a victim who triumphed over adversity, she represented the divine in all people. She refuted the materialists of the time, proving that the soul was indeed real. Notice the terms I use above: *blessing, consummate example, represented the divine in all people,* and *soul was indeed real.* Living up to these terms are heavy burdens for one person to carry! By putting Keller on a pedestal, we understand how audiences perceived her, but we lose the real human being.

I contend that the public's perception of Keller as a perfect, pure victim relates to the public's inability to criticize her. As I discussed in the last chapter, Keller's critics cast her as a victim and charged Sullivan and others instead. Since people cannot criticize icons, they need scapegoats to blame for qualities that do not fit the perfect picture they are painting. In Keller's case, for example, many critics could not accept socialist, revolutionary ideas coming from this angelic figure. It was easier, instead, to ignore remarks of Keller's that did not fit the hero image and/or dismiss the remarks as unimportant (they were simply related to her concerns about eradicating blindness) and/or blame someone else, such as Sullivan. Especially in our democratic society where underdogs are historically supported, it is difficult to blame a victim. Since Keller was considered a victim, perhaps critics could not hold her accountable for her words and actions. It is not surprising that people criticized Sullivan and others for using this "poor victim," rather than criticizing Keller herself. In dealing with handicapped people, many people focus on disabilities and ignore abilities, viewing disabled people as totally helpless, incomplete creatures. In Keller's time, the situation was even worse than today; many disabled people then were placed in insane asylums. Perhaps some critics did not cast blame on Keller because it seemed unfair to blame an incomplete person for her actions.

Ignoring Keller's expressed request to have a Swedenborgian minister at her funeral fits the pattern I outline here. Perhaps the selfish disregard of Keller's wishes was due, in part, to the fact that some people could not bear the notion of her mortality and ultimate finality. Icons should not die.

Keller was a remarkable woman and an eloquent speaker who demonstrated the power of the human spirit. I think we gain more by viewing her as a real person, complete with strengths and weaknesses, rather than as a God-like figure. Some of her arguments supporting what then were unpopular positions are meritorious. More important, the depth of her view of the world as a conflict between good and evil, with no middle ground, is the nucleus of her belief system.

Helen Keller was an angelic woman, but she was also an activist. She was a refined lady, but she was also a reformer. She was a saintly individual, but she was also a spitfire. We can learn the most from her rhetoric by examining what she really had to say. Let us disregard the mythical aura that surrounds Keller's memory and listen to her speak.

Conclusion

As you did at the beginning of the book, imagine yourself living in a world of darkness and silence. A teacher's hand stretches forth and grips your fingers. This hand touches yours, giving you the gift of language. You not only prove that you can be educated, but you graduate from Radcliffe College cum laude. You become fluent in several languages.

You escape isolation and imprisonment. You are no longer alone. Through speaking, lipreading, Braille, and sign language, you make contact and reciprocally communicate with the outside world. Despite sightless skies and soundless seas, you connect to other people. You belong.

Your senses of smell, touch, and taste also link you with the world. You know your mother is in the room because you smell her perfume. You feel your Teacher's hand and know she is there with you. You taste the fruits of the earth and know you are alive.

Perhaps because your eyes and ears are shut, you have opened up your mind and feel and touch with your soul. On a blank canvas, your inner thoughts create words and images. Your soul possesses perfect senses. In fact, you realize that your inner vision sees and hears more than many sighted, hearing people.

You have a vision of a better tomorrow. You deplore the suffering of humanity and envision a world of peace and harmony. Instead of focusing on your own despair, you decide to devote your life to rectifying the woes of the world, to helping oppressed people everywhere. Just as your Teacher stretched out her hand and touched yours, you stretch out your hand and touch countless others. Through speaking and writing, you work for numerous humanitarian causes and empower the blind, deaf, and other fettered souls. Your spirit and your very existence radiate hope. You inspire disabled people, and you open the eyes and ears of many able-bodied people. You have conquered the night of silence.

This was Helen Keller from the time she learned language at age seven until her death at age eighty-seven, June 1, 1968.

For ye shall go out with joy, and be led forth with peace: the mountains and the hills shall break forth before you into singing, and all the trees of the field shall clap their hands.

—Isaiah 55:12

The First Appearance on the Lecture Platform of

HELEN KELLER

And her Teacher Mrs. Macy (Anne M. Sullivan)

SUBJECT

"The Heart and the Hand," or the Right Use of our Senses

TREMONT TEMPLE, Boston
ONE NIGHT ONLY

MONDAY EVENING, MARCH 24th, at 8:15 P. M.

SEATS, 25c. to $1.50, NOW ON SALE

Keller lecturing in public. Keller spoke on "The Heart and the Hand, or The Right Use of Our Senses." Although this Boston lecture is publicized as Keller's "first appearance," she had spoken in public several times before.

PART TWO

A Voice for Social Reform: Texts of Selected Speeches

Speech at Andover

Andover, Massachusetts, May 1891

Dear friends of Andover, I thank you for the pleasure I have had here, and for the gift I have to take to Tommy from you. I shall never forget this visit, and it will make my mother very happy to hear that you have all been so kind to me. It seems to me the world is full of goodness, beauty and love, and how grateful we must be to our heavenly Father who has given us so much to enjoy. His love and care are written all over the walls of nature. I hope you will all come to South Boston some day and see what the little blind children do, and then go out to the beautiful child's garden and see little Tommy and pretty Willie, the little girl from Texas.

Address of Helen Keller at Mt. Airy

Philadelphia, Pennsylvania, July 8, 1896

If you knew all the joy I feel in being able to speak to you to-day, I think you would have some idea of the value of speech to the deaf, and you would understand why I want every little deaf child in all this great world to have an opportunity to learn to speak. I know that much has been said and written on this subject, and that there is a wide difference of opinion among teachers of the deaf in regard to oral instruction. It seems very strange to me that there should be this difference of opinion; I cannot understand how any one interested in our education can fail to appreciate the satisfaction we feel in being able to express our thoughts in living words. Why, I use speech constantly, and I cannot begin to tell you how much pleasure it gives me to do so. Of course I know that it is not always easy for strangers to understand me, but it will be by and by; and in the meantime I have the unspeakable happiness of knowing that my family and friends rejoice in my ability to speak. My little sister and baby brother love to have me tell them stories in the long summer evenings when I am at home; and my mother and teacher often ask me to read to them from my favourite book. I also discuss the political situation with my dear father, and we decide the most perplexing questions quite as satisfactorily to ourselves as if I could see and hear. So you see what a blessing speech is to me. It brings me into closer and tenderer relationship with those I love, and makes it possible for me to enjoy the sweet companionship of a great many persons from whom I should be entirely cut off if I could not talk.

I can remember the time before I learned to speak, and how I used to struggle to express my thoughts by means of the manual alphabet—how my thoughts used to beat against my finger tips like little birds striving to gain their freedom, until one day Miss Fuller opened wide the prison-door and let them escape. I wonder if she remembers how eagerly and gladly they spread their wings and flew away. Of course, it was not easy at first to fly. The speech-wings were weak and broken, and had lost all the grace and beauty that had once been theirs; indeed, nothing was left save the impulse to fly, but that was something. One can never consent to creep when one feels an impulse to soar. But, nevertheless, it seemed to me sometimes that I could never use my speech-wings as God intended I should use them; there were so many difficulties in the way, so many discouragements; but I kept on trying, knowing that patience and perseverance would win in the end. And while I worked, I built the most beautiful air-castles, and dreamed dreams, the pleasantest of which was of the time when I should talk like other people; and the thought of the pleasure it would give my mother to hear my voice once more, sweetened every effort and made every failure an incentive to try harder next time. So I want to say to those who are trying to learn to speak and those who are teaching them: Be of good cheer. Do not think of to-day's failures, but of the success that may come to-morrow. You have set yourselves a difficult task, but you will succeed if you persevere; and you will find a joy in overcoming obstacles—a delight in climbing rugged paths, which you would perhaps never know if you did not sometime slip backward—if the road was always smooth and pleasant. Remember, no effort that we make to attain something beautiful is ever lost. Sometime, somewhere, somehow we shall find that which we seek. We shall speak, yes, and sing, too, as God intended we should speak and sing.

Our Duties to the Blind

Boston, Massachusetts, January 5, 1904

The annual meeting of this association [The Massachusetts Association for Promoting the Interests of the Adult Blind] gives us another opportunity to discuss among ourselves, and to present to the public, the needs and interests of the adult blind, and I am glad to avail myself of the opportunity. This question of helping the blind to support themselves has been near to my heart for many years, since long before the formation of this society. All I have learned on the subject in the books I have read, I have stored up in my mind against the day when I should be able to turn it to the use of my blind fellows. That day has come.

I have heard that some people think the views I am expressing on this subject, and indeed on all subjects, are not my own, but Miss Sullivan's. If you please, I do very often express Miss Sullivan's ideas, just as to the best of my ability I express ideas which I have been fortunate enough to gather from other wise sources—from the books I have read, from the friends with whom I talk, even from the poets, the prophets, and the sages. It is not strange that some of my ideas come from the wise one with whom I am most intimate and to whom I owe all that I am. I rejoice for myself and for you if Miss Sullivan's ideas are commingled with mine. The more on that account ought what I say to receive your respectful consideration; for Miss Sullivan is acquainted with the work of the blind and the work for the blind. She was blind once herself, and she spent six years in the Perkins Institution. She has since proved a successful teacher of the blind. Other teachers from all over the world have sought her out and exchanged views with her. So Miss Sullivan's ideas on the matter we have to consider are those of an expert. But may I venture to protest I have some ideas of my own? It is true I am still an undergraduate, and I have not had time to study the problems of the blind so deeply as I shall some day. I have, however, thought about these problems, and I know that the time is ripe, nay it has long been ripe, to provide for the adult blind the means of self-support.

The blind are in three classes: first, blind children, who need a common school education; second, the aged and the infirm blind who need to be tenderly cared for; third, the able-bodied blind, who ought to work.

For the first class, blind children, this state has splendidly provided in that great two-million dollar school, the Perkins Institution. The second class, like all other people who are invalid and infirm, must be sheltered in the embrace of many public and private charities. For the third class, healthy adult blind, nothing adequate has been done in this state. They do not want to go to school and read books. They do not want to be fed and clothed and housed by other people. They want to work and support themselves. The betterment of this class is the object of our association. We ask that the State give the adult blind opportunity to earn their own living. We do not approve any system to pauperize them. We are not asking for them a degrading pension or the abstract glories of a higher education. We want them apprenticed to trades, and we want some organized method of helping them to positions after they have learned these trades.

Consider the condition of the idle adult blind from the point of view of their fellow citizens, and from their own point of view. What sort of citizens are they now? They are a public or a private burden, a bad debt, an object of pitying charity, an economic loss. When we ask for them, in the name of Christian philanthropy, we ask equally on the ground of economic good sense. If there were three thousand adult blind in this Commonwealth who could be taught to work, and who are not working, to keep them alive means a burden of ten or twelve thousand dollars every seven days. If each of the three thousand could be taught to work, and earn three dollars a week—surely a low figure—the State would obviously be twenty or twenty-five thousand dollars a week richer. At present the adult blind form a large class who are unremunerative and unprofitable.

Such they are from the point of view of the thoughtful citizen. What are they from their point of view?

Not merely are they blind—that can be borne—but they live in idleness, which is the cruelest, least bearable misery that can be laid upon the human heart. No anguish is keener than the sense of helplessness and self-condemnation which overwhelms them when they find every avenue to activity and usefulness closed to them. If they have been to school, their very education makes their sorrow keener because they know all the more deeply what they have lost. They sit with folded hands as the weary days drag by. They remember the faces they used to see, and the objects of delight which made life good to live, and above all they dream of work that is more satisfying than all the learning, all the pleasures gained by man, work that unites the world in friendly association, cheers solitude, and is the balm of hurt minds. They sit in darkness thinking with pain of the past, and with dread of the future that promises no alleviation of their suffering. They think until they can think no more, and some of them become morbid. The monotony and loneliness of their lives is conceivable only to those who have similar deprivations. I have enjoyed the advantages of the blind who are taught. Yet, I used to feel unhappy many times, because it seemed as if my limitation would prevent me from taking an active part in the work of the world. Never did my heart ache more than when I thought I was not fit to be a useful member of society. Now I have found abundant work, and I ask for no other blessedness.

I have talked with blind students at the institutions for the blind, and I remember the distress and perplexity with which they considered how they should shift for themselves when they graduated. Many of them left school only to go back to poor, bare homes where they could find no means of self-support. For seven, ten or fourteen years they live in the midst of refined surroundings; they enjoy good books, good music, and the society of cultivated people. When their school days are over, they return to homes and conditions which they have outgrown. The institution that has educated them forgets them, unless, perchance, they have sufficient ability to fight their life-battle, single-handed and come out victorious. Institutions are proud of successful graduates. Let us not forget the failures. What benefit do the graduates who fail in the struggle of adult life derive from an education which has not been of a kind that could be turned to practical account? From an economic point of view has the money invested in that education been invested wisely? To teach Latin and Greek and higher mathematics to blind pupils, and not to teach them to earn their bread, is to build a house entirely of stucco, without stones to the walls or rafters to the roof. I have received letters from educated blind people, who repeat the cry, "Give us work, or we perish," and their despair lies heavy on my heart.

It is difficult to get satisfactory statistics about the blind after they graduate from the institutions where they receive a book education, because little or no interest is shown in them after they leave school. It is still harder to get information about the blind who have lost their sight when they are too old to go to the existing institutions. But it is evident that only a small portion of the blind now support themselves. A prominent teacher of the blind is reported to have said that less than 8 per cent, of the entire blind population of the United States, are self-supporting, and the percentage for the whole country will be higher than the percentage for this State; for Massachusetts is behind some states in industrial education for the blind. Others will give you the exact figures. But whether there are in Massachusetts one thousand or five thousand adult blind who might be taught to work, they are too many for us to have neglected so long.

It is difficult to understand how a State which was a pioneer in the education of the blind, and which boasts the Perkins Institution, could have so conspicuously failed to turn their education to account. Surely it is only an accidental division which has left one side of the education of the blind in the sunlight where Doctor Howe placed it, and has left the other side in the dark. In spirit, all aspects of the education of the blind are one, and we can be sure that Doctor Howe, had he lived, would have been the leader of this movement, in which we are doing our little best. Indeed, I believe that he would long ago have rendered our labours unnecessary. Let us gratefully and lovingly render, in company with those who survive him, the honour that is his due. But since he is dead and cannot lead us, let us push forward, guided by what light we have. Wisdom did not die with Solomon. All knowledge about the needs and capabilities of the blind did not die with Doctor Howe. There is much to do which he did not live to achieve, or, it may even be, which he had not thought of.

The most important fact remains that nothing of consequence has been done in Massachusetts since Doctor Howe's day. It was he who established the workshop for the adult blind in South Boston, in connection with the Perkins Institution, and that remains much as he left it. Two or three years ago, the State appropriated a small sum of money—five thousand dollars, I think—for travelling teachers, who visit the homes of blind persons too old to go to Perkins Institution. This was a step in the right direction, but it was inadequate, and it is not altogether practical. I have known old ladies who have told me how glad they were to learn to read the Lord's Prayer with their fingers. They looked forward to the weekly lesson with joy; it was a bright spot in the monotony of their life. But, after all, this is not so important as it is to teach younger and stronger men and women to earn their living. The needs of the adult blind cannot be covered by an extension of this appropriation or by a development of this kind of teaching. Something new is necessary. Either the scope of the workshop at South Boston must be greatly enlarged, or new ones, independent of it, must be established. It would have been no argument against founding the Massachusetts Institute of Technology to use that there was already a good college across the Charles. He who is content with what has been done is an obstacle in the path of progress.

Up! Up! Something must be done. We have delayed too long. If you want to know how long we have delayed, listen to what the Bishop of Ripon said recently at the Institution for the Blind in Bradford, England. Speaking of a time thirty years ago, he said: "The work-house and the charity of the passer-by in the street were the only hope of the blind. All that has been changed. The blind have been taught useful occupations, and have been enabled in many cases to earn sufficient to maintain themselves in comfort, so that it has come to be a reproach that a blind man or woman should beg in the streets." This is the change in England in thirty years. There has been no such change in Massachusetts. Something must be done, that is clear. What shall we do?

There are two things to do which work together and become one. First, let the State establish by an adequate appropriation an agency for the employment of the blind. This agency should be in Boston. At the head of it should be a competent man, whose sole duty should be to study all occupations in which the blind can engage, to exhibit the work of the blind, to advise and encourage them, and to bring employers and blind employees together without expense to either. This bureau should do for the blind of Massachusetts what is done by the employment bureau of the British and Foreign Blind Association in England, namely, provide a place in the busiest part of the city, where blind workers and their patrons can be brought together and where articles made by the blind can be advantageously exhibited. The agent should advertise to the public that they can get blind piano tuners, notepaper embossers, shampooers, masseurs, chairmakers, brushmakers, tutors, singers, church organists, tea tasters, and other useful blind people.

Then there is the second part of the work—to increase the variety and efficiency of those other useful blind workers. This means industrial schools; that is, workshops, with all possible machinery and appliances which the blind can profitably handle. To every blind person should be given opportunity to serve an industrial apprenticeship. After he has learned this trade, or that mechanical process, he would go to the agent at the employment bureau, or the agent would go to him, and the agent would then offer to employers the services of a blind workman. In each of the large manufacturing towns—Brockton, Lowell, Taunton, Lawrence, Worcester—there should be a branch of the agency. The head of each branch bureau should know all the industries peculiar to his locality, and should know the employers of the neighborhood.

Suppose at the age of thirty a man loses his sight, and that means that he must give up his work, let us say, as salesman in a dry-goods house. He goes to the nearest agent of the Massachusetts Industrial Bureau for the Blind. The agent knows every occupation in the State which it is profitable for a blind man to engage in, and he tells this man that the best occupation near his home is running a machine of a certain kind. The man then goes to the Industrial School for the Blind and learns to run that machine; in other words he serves an apprenticeship in a free state school, and incidentally learns the other things which a blind man must learn in order to adapt himself to the new conditions of his life; that is, he gets the experience of being blind. At the end of the apprenticeship the agent, knowing what the man can do, goes to a manufacturer and asks that he give the man a chance. The agent stands behind the man during his period of probation, until the employer is convinced that his blind workman understands his business.

Am I dreaming dreams? It is no untried experiment. It is being done in Great Britain. Remember that to educate a blind man so that he becomes a competent workman is no magical and mysterious process. A blind man can do nothing less and nothing more than what a person with five senses can do, minus what can be done only with the eye. Remember, too, that when a man loses his sight he does not know himself what he can do. He needs some one of experience to advise him. The other day the commission listened to a blind man, forty years old, who lost his sight at the age of thirty-six, four years ago. Before he became blind, he had been a lithographer, and was for eight years a foreman. He testified that he was determined not to be a quitter, and that he had tried one and another kind of work, only to fail in each. "What," asked one of the commissioners, "do you think you can learn to do?" "I do not know," replied the man. Do we need a stronger argument for an industrial agency than this answer? Although intelligent and industrious, this man had struggled wildly in the dark for four years, trying in vain to discover what kind of work he had best apply himself to. Think of it! In four years he had had no one to tell him what it was best for him to try to learn to do.

Now who shall change all this? Who shall establish the Massachusetts Industrial Bureau for the Blind? Surely the State—Massachusetts, in whose watchtowers burn continuously the beacons of sympathy and love; Massachusetts, to whom every State in our country turns for example and guidance in education and philanthropy; Massachusetts, in whose beneficent institutions the deaf have learned to speak, the blind to read the printed page, the idiot clay to think. Surely Massachusetts will not now turn a deaf ear to the cry of the helpless adult blind. Has she not lovingly nurtured and abundantly provided for the Perkins Institution and the Kindergarten for the Blind? Once the people learn what should be done, we need not fear that those whose authority is law and those whose authority is loving charity will neglect the sacred duty to raise the adult blind from dependence to self-respecting citizenship. Therefore I have complete faith in the ultimate triumph of our cause.

The Heaviest Burden of the Blind

New York City, January 15, 1907

It is a great pleasure to me to speak in New York about the blind. For New York is great because of the open hand with which it responds to the needs of the weak and the poor. The men and women for whom I speak are poor and weak in that they lack one of the chief weapons with which the human being fights his battle. But they must not on that account be sent to the rear. Much less must they be pensioned like disabled children. They must be kept in the fight for their own sake, and for the sake of the strong. It is a blessing to the strong to give help to the weak. Otherwise there would be no excuse for having the poor always with us.

The help we give the unfortunate must be intelligent. Charity may flow freely and yet fail to touch the deserts of human life. Disorganized charity is creditable to the heart but not to the mind. Pity and tears make poetry; but they do not raise model tenement houses, or save the manhood of blind men. The heaviest burden on the blind is not blindness, but idleness, and they can be relieved of this greater burden.

Our work for the blind is practical. The Massachusetts commission, your association, and the New York commission are placing it on a sincere basis. The first task is to make a careful census of the blind, to find out how many there are, how old they are, what are their circumstances, when they lost their sight and from what cause. Without such a census there can be no order in our work. In Massachusetts this task is nearly completed.

The next step is to awaken each town and city to a sense of its duty to the blind. For it is the community where the blind man lives that ultimately determines his success or his failure. The State can teach him to work, supply him with raw materials, and capital to start his business; but his fellow-citizens must furnish the market for his products, and give him the encouragement without which no blind man can make headway. They must do more than this; they must meet him with a sympathy that conforms to the dignity of his manhood and his capacity for service. Indeed, the community should regard it as a disgrace for the blind to beg on the street corner, or receive unearned pensions.

It is not helpful—in the long run it is harmful—to buy worthless articles of the blind. For many years kind-hearted people have bought futile and childish things because the blind made them. Quantities of beadwork, that can appeal to no eye save the eye of pity, have passed as specimens of the work of the blind. If beadwork had been studied in the schools for the blind and supervised by competent seeing persons, it could have been made a profitable industry for the sightless. I have examined beautiful beadwork in the shops—purses, bags, belts, lampshades, and dress-trimmings—some of it very expensive—imported from France and Germany. Under proper supervision this beadwork could be made by the blind. This is only one example of the sort of manufacture that the blind may profitably engage in.

One of the principal objects of the movement which we ask you to help is to promote good workmanship among the sightless. In Boston, in a fashionable shopping district, the Massachusetts commission has opened a salesroom where the best handicraft of all the sightless in the State may be exhibited and sold. There are hand-woven curtains, table-covers, bed-spreads, sofa-pillows, linen suits, rugs; and the articles are of good design and workmanship. People buy them not out of pity for the maker, but out of admiration for the thing. Orders have already come from Minnesota, from England, from Egypt. So the blind of the New World have sent light into Egyptian darkness!

This shop is under the same roof with the salesroom of the Perkins Institution for the Blind. The old school and the new commission are working side by side. I desire to see similar cooperation between the New York Institution for the Blind and the New York Association. The true vale of a school for the sightless is not merely to enlighten intellectual darkness, but to lend a hand to every movement in the interests of the blind. It is not enough that our blind children receive a common-school education. They should do something well enough to become wage-earners. When they are properly educated, they desire to work more than they desire ease or entertainment. If some of the blind are ambitionless and lazy, the fault lies partly with those who have directed their education, partly with our indolent progenitors in the Garden of Eden. All over the land the blind are stretching forth eager hands to the new tasks which shall soon be within their reach. They embrace labour gladly because they know it is strength.

One of our critics has suggested that we who call the blind forth to toil are as one who should overload a disabled horse and compel him to earn his oats. In the little village where I live, there was a lady so mistakenly kind to a pet horse that she never broke him to harness, and fed him twelve quarts of oats a day. The horse had to be shot. I am not afraid that we shall kill our blind with kindness. I am still less afraid that we shall break their backs.

Nay, I can tell you of blind men who of their own accord enter the sharp competition of business and put their hands zealously to the tools of trade. It is our part to train them in business, to teach them to use their tools skillfully. Before this association was thought of, blind men had given examples of energy and industry, and with such examples shining in the dark other blind men will not be content to be numbered among those who will not, or cannot, carry burden on shoulder or tool in hand—those who know not the honour of hard-won independence.

The new movement for the blind rests on a foundation of common sense. It is not the baseless fabric of a sentimentalist's dream. We do not believe that the blind should be segregated from the seeing, gathered together in a sort of Zion City, as has been done in Roumania and attempted in Iowa. We have no queen to preside over such a city. America is a democracy, a multimonarchy, and the city of the blind is everywhere. Each community should take care of its own blind, provide employment for them, and enable them to work side by side with the seeing. We do not expect to find among the blind a disproportionate number of geniuses. Education does not develop in them remarkable talent. Like the seeing man, the blind man may be a philosopher, a mathematician, a linguist, a seer, a poet, a prophet. But believe me, if the light of genius burns within him, it will burn despite his infirmity, and not because of it. The lack of one sense—or two—never helped a human being. We should be glad of the sixty or the sixteenth sense with which our friends and the newspaper reporters, more generous than nature, are wont to endow us. To paraphrase Mr. Kipling, we are not heroes and we are not cowards too. We are ordinary folk limited by an extraordinary incapacity. If we do not always succeed in our undertakings, even with assistance from friends, we console ourselves with the thought that in the vast company of the world's failures is many a sound pair of eyes!

I appeal to you, give the blind man the assistance that shall secure for him complete or partial independence. He is blind and falters. Therefore go a little more than half-way to meet him. Remember, however brave and self-reliant he is, he will always need a guiding hand in his.

The Conservation of Eyesight

Boston, Massachusetts, February 14, 1911

I rejoice that the greatest of all work for the blind—the saving of eyesight—has been so clearly laid before the public. The reports of progress in the conservation of eyes, of health, of life, and of all things precious to man, are as a trumpet blast summoning us to still greater effort. The devotion of physicians and laymen and the terrible needs of our fellow-men ought to hearten us in the fight against conquerable misery.

Our worst foes are ignorance, poverty, and the unconscious cruelty of our commercial society. These are the causes of blindness; these are the enemies which destroy the sight of children and workmen and undermine the health of mankind. So long as these enemies remain unvanquished, so long will there be blind and crippled men and women.

To study the diseases and accidents which cause loss of sight, and to learn how the surgeon can prevent or alleviate them, is not enough. We should strive to put an end to the conditions which produce the diseases and accidents.

This case of blindness, the physician says, resulted from ophthalmia. It was really caused by a dark, overcrowded room, by the indecent herding together of human beings in unsanitary tenements. We are told that another case of blindness resulted from the bursting of a wheel. The true cause was an employer's failure to safeguard his machine. Investigations show that there are many ingenious safeguards for machinery which are not adopted because their adoption would diminish the manufacturer's profits. We Americans have been slow, dishonourably slow, in taking measures for the protection of our workmen.

Does it occur to any of you that the white lace which we wear is darkened by the failing eyes of the maker? The trouble is that most of us don't understand the essential relation between poverty and disease. I do not believe that there is any one in this City of Kind Hearts who would willingly receive dividends if he knew that they had been paid in part with blinded eyes and broken backs. If you doubt that there is any such connection between our prosperity and the sorrows of others, consult those bare but illuminating reports of industrial commissions and labour bureaus. They are less eloquent than oratory, less pleasant than fiction, but more convincing than either. In them you will find the fundamental causes of much blindness and crookedness, of shrunken limbs and degraded minds. These causes must be further searched out, and every condition in which blindness breeds must be exposed and abolished. Let our battlecry be, "No preventable disease, no unnecessary poverty, no blinding ignorance among mankind."

The Gift of Speech

New York City, April 8, 1913

I am glad that so many intelligent people are interested in helping the deaf to speak. You have asked me to come here and tell you how you can help in a work that is near to my heart. I am happy to stand before you, myself an example of what may be done to open dumb lips and liberate mute voices. I was dumb, now I speak. Intelligent instruction and the devotion of others wrought this miracle in me. What has been done for me can be done for others. You can all help the deaf child. You can help him by being interested in his struggle. You know now, if you have not known before, that he can learn to speak, and you can spread the knowledge that shall save him.

What the world needs is enlightened understanding on many subjects. There are plenty of brains and plenty of good-will in the world. All that we need is to put them together. We must put thought and understanding into our efforts to help people. So much time and money are wasted every day because we do not get to the root of our difficulties!

In the case of the deaf, physicians and parents often retard the development of deaf children because they do not realize the necessity of an early start. When the physician knows that the organ of hearing is permanently impaired, the child should be placed under the guidance of a skillful teacher, even while there may still be hope of improvement. Nothing can be lost by beginning his education at once. Should he be fortunate enough to recover his hearing later, in the meantime the years will have been spent educationally. If lifelong deafness is his lot, he will have had the advantages of a prompt beginning. The psychological period for the acquisition of speech and language will not have been lost, and the difficulty of teaching him will be lessened, and the result will be far more satisfactory.

Speech is the birthright of every child. It is the deaf child's one fair chance to keep in touch with his fellows. In many ways deafness is a greater disaster than blindness. Blindness robs the day of its light and makes us dependent and physically helpless. Deafness stops up the fountain-head of knowledge and turns life into a desert. For without language intellectual life is impossible. Try to imagine what it means to be deaf and dumb. Perpetual silence, silence full of longing to be understood, to speak, to hear the voices of our loved ones; silence that starves the mind, fetters the spirit and adds still another burden to labour.

Deafness, like poverty, stunts and deadens its victims, until they do not realize the wretchedness of their condition. They are incapable of desiring improvement. God help them! They grope, they stumble with their eyes wide open, they are indifferent. They miss everything in the world that makes life worth living, and yet they do not realize their own bondage. We must not wait for the deaf to ask for speech, or for the submerged of humanity to rise up and demand their liberties. We who see, we who hear, we who understand must help them, must give them the bread of knowledge, must teach them what their human inheritance is. Let every science do its part—medicine, surgery, otology, psychology, education, invention, economics, mechanics. And while you are working for the deaf child, do not forget that his problem is only part of a greater problem, the problem of bettering the condition of all mankind. Let us here and now resolve that every deaf child shall have a chance to speak, and that every man shall have a fair opportunity to make the best of himself. Then shall we mend the broken lyre of human speech and lessen the deafness and blindness of the world.

A New Light Is Coming

Sagamore Beach, Massachusetts, July 8, 1913

D ear Friends: I came here to listen, not to talk. I have not prepared a speech. But I suppose a woman can always think of something to say. If other subjects fail, one can talk about oneself.

Ever since I came here, people have been asking my friends how I can have a first-hand knowledge of the subjects you are discussing. They seem to think that one deaf and blind cannot know about the world of people, of ideas, of facts. Well, I plead guilty to the charge that I am deaf and blind, though I forget the fact most of the time. It is true, I cannot hear my neighbors discussing the questions of the day. But, judging from what is repeated to me of their discussions, I feel that I do not miss much. I can read. I can read the views of well-informed thinkers like Alfred Russell Wallace, Sir Oliver Lodge, Ruskin, H. G. Wells, Bernard Shaw, Karl Lautsky, Darwin and Karl Marx. Besides books, I have magazines in raised print published in America, England, France, Germany and Austria.

Of course, I am not always on the spot when things happen, nor are you. I did not witness the dreadful accident at Stamford the other day, nor did you, nor did most people in the United States. But that did not prevent me, any more than it prevented you, from knowing about it.

To be sure, I have never been a captain of industry, or a soldier, or a strikebreaker. But I have studied these professions, and I think I understand their relation to society. At all events, I claim my right to discuss them. I have the advantage of a mind trained to think, and that is the difference between myself and most people, not my blindness and their sight. It seems to me that they are blind indeed who do not see that there must be something very wrong when the workers—the men and women who produce the wealth of the nation—are ill paid, ill fed, ill clothed, ill housed. Deaf indeed are they who do not hear the desperation in the voice of the people crying out against cruel poverty and social injustice. Dull indeed are their hearts who turn their backs upon misery and support a system that grinds the life and soul out of men and women.

I have been much interested in what I have heard here. I am glad so many of you have your eyes open to the questions of the day, and to the great change that is taking place in the structure of society. There is always hope of improvement when people are willing to try to understand. The change will take place whether we understand or not. Comrade Giovannitti has explained to you how he believes that great change is coming. If you understood him, you will see that it is the workers themselves who will work out their own salvation. All we can do is to get into the procession.

We are marching toward a new freedom. We are learning that freedom is the only safe condition to human beings, men and women and children. Only through freedom, freedom for all, can we hope for a true democracy. Some of us have imagined that we live in a democracy. We do not. A democracy would mean equal opportunity for all. It would mean that every child had a chance to be well born, well fed, well taught and properly started in life. It would mean that every woman had a voice in the making of the laws under which she lives. It would mean that all men enjoyed the fruits of their labor. Such a democracy has never existed.

But some of us are waking up. We are finding out what is wrong with the world. We are going to make it right. We are learning that we live by each other, and that the life for each other is the only life worth living. A new light is coming to millions who looked for light and found darkness, a life to them who looked for the grave, and were bitter in spirit. We are part of this light. Let us go forth from here shafts of the sun unto shadows. With our hearts let us see, with your hands let us break every chain. Then, indeed, shall we know a better and nobler humanity. For there will be no more slaves. Men will not go on strike for 50 cents more a week. Little children will not have to starve or work in mill and factory. Motherhood will no longer be a sorrow. We shall be "just one great family of friends and brothers."

Menace of the Militarist Program

New York City, December 19, 1915

The burden of war always falls heaviest on the toilers. They are taught that their masters can do no wrong, and go out in vast numbers to be killed on the battlefield. And what is their reward? If they escape death they come back to face heavy taxation and have their burden of poverty doubled. Through all the ages they have been robbed of the just rewards of their patriotism as they have been of the just reward of their labor.

The only moral virtue of war is that it compels the capitalist system to look itself in the face and admit it is a fraud. It compels the present society to admit that it has no morals it will not sacrifice for gain. During a war, the sanctity of a home, and even of private property is destroyed. Governments do what it is said the "crazy Socialists" would do if in power.

In spite of the historical proof of the futility of war, the United States is preparing to raise a billion dollars and a million soldiers in preparation for war. Behind the active agitators for defense you will find J. P. Morgan & Co., and the capitalists who have invested their money in shrapnel plants, and others that turn out implements of murder. They want armaments because they beget war, for these capitalists want to develop new markets for their hideous traffic.

I look upon the whole world as my fatherland, and every war has to me a horror of a family freud. I look upon true patriotism as the brotherhood of man and the service of all to all. The only fighting that saves is the one that helps the world toward liberty, justice and an abundant life for all.

To prepare this nation in the true sense of the word, not for war, but for peace and happiness, the State should govern every department of industry, health and education in such a way as to maintain the bodies and minds of the people in soundness and efficiency. Then, the nation will be prepared to withstand the demand to fight for a perpetuation of its own slavery at the bidding of a tyrant.

After all, the best preparation is one that disarms the hostility of other nations and makes friends of them. Nothing is to be gained by the workers from war. Their wages are not increased, nor their toil made lighter, nor their homes made more comfortable. The army they are supposed to raise can be used to break strikes as well as defend the people.

If the democratic measures of preparedness fall before the advance of a world empire, the worker has nothing to fear. No conqueror can beat down his wages more ruthlessly or oppress him more than his own fellow citizens of the capitalist world are doing. The worker has nothing to lose but his chains, and he has a world to win. He can win it at one stroke from a world empire. We must form a fully equipped, militant international union so that we can take possession of such a world empire.

This great republic is a mockery of freedom as long as you are doomed to dig and sweat to earn a miserable living while the masters enjoy the fruit of your toil. What have you to fight for? National independence? That means the masters' independence. The laws that send you to jail when you demand better living conditions? The flag? Does it wave over a country where you are free and have a home, or does it rather symbolize a country that meets you with clenched fists when you strike for better wages and shorter hours? Will you fight for your masters' religion which teaches you to obey them even when they tell you to kill one another?

Why don't you make a junk heap of your master's religion, his civilization, his kings and his customs that tend to reduce a man to a brute and God to a monster? Let there go forth a clarion call for liberty. Let the workers form one great world-wide union, and let there be a globe-encircling revolt to gain for the workers true liberty and happiness.

Strike Against War

New York City, January 5, 1916

To begin with, I have a word to say to my good friends, the editors, and others who are moved to pity me. Some people are grieved because they imagine I am in the hands of unscrupulous persons who lead me astray and persuade me to espouse unpopular causes and make me the mouthpiece of their propaganda. Now, let it be understood once and for all that I do not want their pity; I would not change places with one of them. I know what I am talking about. My sources of information are as good and reliable as anybody else's. I have papers and magazines from England, France, Germany and Austria that I can read myself. Not all the editors I have met can do that. They are an overworked, misunderstood class. Let them remember, though, that if I cannot see the fire at the end of their cigarettes, neither can they thread a needle in the dark. All I ask, gentleman, is a fair field and no favor. I have entered the fight against preparedness and against the economic system under which we live. It is to be a fight to the finish, and I ask no quarter.

The future of the world rests in the hands of America. The future of America rests on the backs of 80,000,000 working men and women and their children. We are facing a grave crisis in our national life. The few who profit from the labor of the masses want to organize the workers into an army which will protect the interests of the capitalists. You are urged to add to the heavy burdens you already bear the burden of a larger army and many additional warships. It is in your power to refuse to carry the artillery and the dreadnoughts and to shake off some of the burdens, too, such as limousines, steam yachts and country estates. You do not need to make a great noise about it. With the silence and dignity of creators you can end wars and the system of selfishness and exploitation that causes wars. All you need to do to bring about this stupendous revolution is to straighten up and fold your arms.

We are not preparing to defend our country. Even if we were as helpless as Congressman Gardner says we are, we have no enemies foolhardy enough to attempt to invade the United States. The talk about attack from Germany and Japan is absurd. Germany has its hands full and will be busy with its own affairs for some generations after the European war is over.

With full control of the Atlantic Ocean and the Mediterranean Sea, the allies failed to land enough men to defeat the Turks at Gallipoli; and then they failed again to land an army at Salonica in time to check the Bulgarian invasion of Serbia. The conquest of America by water is a nightmare confined exclusively to ignorant persons and members of the Navy League.

Yet, everywhere, we hear fear advanced as argument for armament. It reminds me of a fable I read. A certain man found a horseshoe. His neighbor began to weep and wail because, as he justly pointed out, the man who found the horseshoe might someday find a horse. Having found the shoe, he might shoe him. The neighbor's child might some day go so near the horse's heels as to be kicked, and die. Undoubtedly the two families would quarrel and fight, and several valuable lives would be lost through the finding of the horseshoe. You know the last war we had we quite accidentally picked up some islands in the Pacific Ocean which may some day be the cause of a quarrel between ourselves and Japan. I'd rather drop those islands right now and forget about them than go to war to keep them. Wouldn't you?

Congress is not preparing to defend the people of the United States. It is planning to protect the capital of American speculators and investors in Mexico, South America, China and the Philippine Islands. Incidentally this preparation will benefit the manufacturers of munitions and war machines.

Until recently there were uses in the United States for the money taken from the workers. But American labor is exploited almost to the limit now, and our national resources have all been appropriated. Still, the profits keep piling up new capital. Our flourishing industry in implements of murder is filling the vaults of New York's banks with gold. And a dollar that is not being used to make a slave of some human being is not fulfilling its purpose in the capitalistic scheme. That dollar must be invested in South America, Mexico, China, or the Philippines.

It was no accident that the Navy League came into prominence at the same time that the National City Bank of New York established a branch in Buenos Aires. It is not a mere coincidence that six business associates of J. P. Morgan are officials of defense leagues. And chance did not dictate that Mayor Mitchel should appoint to his Committee of Safety a thousand men that represent a fifth of the wealth of the United States. These men want their foreign investments protected.

Every modern war has had its roots in exploitation. The Civil War was fought to decide whether the slaveholders of the South or the capitalists of the North should exploit the West. The Spanish-American War decided that the United States should exploit Cuba and the Philippines. The South African War decided that the British should exploit the diamond mines. The Russo-Japanese War decided that Japan should exploit Korea. The present war is to decide who shall exploit the Balkans, Turkey, Persia, Egypt, India, China, Africa. And we are whetting our sword to scare the victors into sharing the spoils with us. Now, the workers are not interested in the spoils; they will not get any of them anyway.

The preparedness propagandists have still another object, and a very important one. They want to give the people something to think about besides their own unhappy condition. They know the cost of living is high, wages are low, employment is uncertain and will be much more so when the European call for munitions stops. No matter how hard and incessantly the people work, they often cannot afford the comforts of life; many cannot obtain the necessities.

Every few days we are given a new war scare to lend realism to their propaganda. They have had us on the verge of war over the *Lusitania,* the *Gulflight,* the *Ancona,* and now they want the workingmen to become excited over the sinking of the *Persia.* The workingman has no interest in any of these ships. The Germans might sink every vessel on the Atlantic Ocean and the Mediterranean Sea, and kill Americans with every one—the American workingman would still have no reason to go to war.

All the machinery of the system has been set in motion. Above the complaint and din of the protest from the workers is heard the voice of authority.

"Friends," it says, "fellow workmen, patriots; your country is in danger! There are foes on all sides of us. There is nothing between us and our enemies except the Pacific Ocean and the Atlantic Ocean. Look at what has happened to Belgium. Consider the fate of Serbia. Will you murmur about low wages when your country, your very liberties, are in jeopardy? What are the miseries you endure compared to the humiliation of having a victorious German army sail up the East River? Quit your whining, get busy and prepare to defend your firesides and your flag. Get an army, get a navy; be ready to meet the invaders like the loyal-hearted freemen you are."

Will the workers walk into this trap? Will they be fooled again? I am afraid so. The people have always been amenable to oratory of this sort. The workers know they have no enemies except their masters. They know that their citizenship papers are no warrant for the safety of themselves or their wives and children. They know that honest sweat, persistent toil and years of struggle bring them nothing worth holding on to, worth fighting for. Yet, deep down in their foolish hearts they believe they have a country. Oh blind vanity of slaves?

The clever ones, up in the high places know how childish and silly the workers are. They know that if the government dresses them up in khaki and gives them a rifle and starts them off with a brass band and waving banners, they will go forth to fight valiantly for their own enemies. They are taught that brave men die for their country's honor. What a price to pay for an abstraction—the lives of millions of young men; other millions crippled and blinded for life; existence made hideous for still more millions of human beings; the achievement and inheritance of generations swept away in a moment—and nobody better off for all the misery! This terrible sacrifice would be comprehensible if the thing you die for and call country fed, clothed, housed and warmed you, educated and cherished your children. I think the workers are the most unselfish of the children of men; they toil and live and die for other people's country, other people's sentiments, other people's liberties and other people's happiness! The workers have no liberties of their own; they are not free when they are compelled to work twelve or ten or eight hours a day. They are not free when they are ill paid for their exhausting toil. They are not free when their children must labor in mines, mills and factories or starve, and when their women may be driven by poverty to lives of shame. They are not free when they are clubbed and imprisoned because they go on strike for a raise of wages and for the elemental justice that is their right as human beings.

We are not free unless the men who frame and execute the laws represent the interests of the lives of the people and no other interest. The ballot does not make a free man out of a wage slave. There has never existed a truly free and democratic nation in the world. From time immemorial men have followed with blind loyalty the strong men who had the power of money and of armies. Even while battlefields were piled high with their own dead they have tilled the lands of the rulers and have been robbed of the fruits of their labor. They have built palaces and pyramids, temples and cathedrals that held no real shrine of liberty.

As civilization has grown more complex the workers have become more and more enslaved, until today they are little more than parts of the machines they operate. Daily they face the dangers of railroad, bridge, skyscraper, freight train, stokehold, stockyard, lumber raft and mine. Panting and straining at the docks, on the railroads and underground and on the seas, they move the traffic and pass from land to land the precious commodities that make it possible for us to live. And what is their reward? A scanty wage, often poverty, rents, taxes, tributes and war indemnities.

The kind of preparedness the workers want is reorganization and reconstruction of their whole life, such as has never been attempted by statesmen or governments. The Germans found out years ago that they could not raise good soldiers in the slums so they abolished the slums. They saw to it that all the people had at least a few of the essentials of civilization—decent lodging, clean streets, wholesome if scanty food, proper medical care and proper safeguards for the workers in their occupations. That is only a small part of what should be done, but what wonders that one step toward the right sort of preparedness has wrought for Germany! For eighteen months it has kept itself free from invasion while carrying on an extended war of conquest, and its armies are still pressing on with unabated vigor. It is your business to force these reforms on the Administration. Let there be no more talk about what a government can or cannot do. All these things have been done by all the belligerent nations in the hurly-burly of war. Every fundamental industry has been managed better by the governments than by private corporations.

It is your duty to insist upon still more radical measures. It is your business to see that no child is employed in an industrial establishment or mine or store, and that no worker is needlessly exposed to accident or disease. It is your business to make them give you clean cities, free from smoke, dirt and congestion. It is your business to make them pay you a living wage. It is your business to see that this kind of preparedness is carried into every department of the nation, until every one has a chance to be well born, well nourished, rightly educated, intelligent and serviceable to the country at all times.

Strike against all ordinances and laws and institutions that continue the slaughter of peace and the butcheries of war. Strike against war, without you no battles can be fought. Strike against manufacturing shrapnel and gas bombs and other tools of murder. Strike against preparedness that means death and misery to millions of human beings. Be not dumb, obedient slaves in an army of destruction. Be heroes in an army of construction.

Onward, Comrades!

New York City, December 31, 1920

The hour has struck for the Grand March! Onward, comrades, all together! Fall in line! Start the New Year with a cheer! Let us join the world's procession marching toward a glad tomorrow. Strong of hope and brave in heart the West shall meet the East! March with us, brothers every one! March with us to all things new! Climb with us the hills of God to a wider, holier life. Onward, comrades, all together, onward to meet the dawn!

Leave behind your doubts and fears! What need have we for "ifs" and "buts?" Away with parties, schools and leagues! Get together, keep in step, shoulder to shoulder, hearts throbbing as one! Face the future, outdaring all you have dared! March on, O comrades, strong and free, out of darkness, out of silence, out of hate and custom's deadening sway! Onward, comrades, all together, onward to the wind-blown dawn!

With us shall go the new day, shining behind the dark. With us shall go power, knowledge, justice, truth. The time is full! A new world awaits us. Its fruits, its joys, its opportunities are ours for the taking! Fear not the hardships of the road—the storm, the parching heat or winter's cold, hunger or thirst or ambushed foe! There are bright lights ahead of us, leave the shadows behind! In the East a new star is risen! With pain and anguish the old order has given birth to the new, and behold in the East a man-child is born! Onward, comrades, all together! Onward to the campfires of Russia! Onward to the coming dawn!

Through the night of our despair rings the keen call of the new day. All the powers of darkness could not still the shout of joy in faraway Moscow! Meteor-like through the heavens flashed the golden words of light, "Soviet Republic of Russia." Words sun-like piercing the dark, joyous radiant love-words banishing hate, bidding the teeming world of men to wake and live! Onward, comrades, all together, onward to the bright, redeeming dawn!

With peace and brotherhood make sweet the bitter way of men! Today and all the days to come, repeat the words of Him who said, "Thou shalt not kill." Send on psalming winds the angel chorus, "Peace on earth, good-will to men." Onward march, and keep on marching until

His will on earth is done! Onward, comrades, all together, onward to the life-giving fountain of dawn!

All along the road beside us throng the peoples sad and broken, weeping women, children hungry, homeless like little birds cast out of their nest. Onward march, comrades, strong to lift and save! With their hearts aflame, untamed, glorying in martyrdom they hail us passing quickly. "Halt not, O comrades, yonder glimmers the star of our hope, the red-centered dawn in the East! Halt not, lest you perish ere you reach the land of promise." Onward, comrades, all together, onward to the sun-red dawn!

We march through trackless wilds of hate and death, across earth's battlefields. O comrades, pause one panting moment and shed a tear for the youth of the world, killed in its strength and beauty—our brothers, our comrades tenderly loved, the valiant young men of all lands eagerly seeking life's great enterprises, love, adventure and the fair country of bright dreams. Under our feet they lie, mingling their clean young flesh with the soil, the rain and the heat! Over our murdered dead we march to the new day. Onward, comrades, all together, onward to the spirit's unquenchable dawn!

The Vaudeville Circuit, 1919–24

From 1919 until 1924, Keller joined the Vaudeville Circuit. In addition to several shorter trips, she and Teacher made two tours across the continental United States. The Vaudeville Circuit took them to many cities, including Mount Vernon, New York City, Baltimore, Pittsburgh, Buffalo, Providence, Chicago, Cleveland, Des Moines, Hot Springs, Tulsa, San Francisco, Los Angeles, and Seattle.

The act lasted twenty minutes. First, Teacher explained how Helen had learned language. Then, Keller gave a brief speech. Finally, listeners asked questions. Teacher "spoke" the questions into Keller's hands, which Keller answered with a quick wit and a sharp tongue.

Although Keller's answers appeared spontaneous, she really had prepared most of them beforehand. She created a seventeen page list of the most frequently asked questions and her replies.

On the Vaudeville Circuit, Keller revealed different sides of her personality than she had shown in her public speeches. Her lively sallies demonstrated her sense of humor. Several answers presented her liberal political leanings, views far to the left of her Teacher.

Some Prepared Answers to Frequently Asked Questions

Q. Which is the greatest affliction, deafness, dumbness, blindness?
A. None.
Q. What then is the greatest human affliction?
A. Boneheadedness.
Q. Do you think any government wants peace?
A. The policy of governments is to seek peace and pursue war.
Q. What is your definition of a Bolshevik?
A. Anyone whose opinions you particularly dislike.
Q. Who are the three greatest men of our time?
A. Lenin, Edison, and Charlie Chaplin.
Q. What do you think of Soviet Russia?
A. Soviet Russia is the first organized attempt of the workers to establish an order of society in which human life and happiness shall be of the first importance, and not the conservation of property for a privileged class.

Q. Who do you think are the most unhappy people?

A. People who have nothing to do.

Q. What brings the greatest satisfaction?

A. Work, accomplishment.

Q. What do you think of Mr. Harding?

A. I have a fellow-feeling for him; he seems as blind as I am.

Q. Can you think of any tax that people would willingly pay?

A. Yes, a tax on millionaires.

Q. What did America gain by the war?

A. The American Legion and a bunch of other troubles.

Q. Do you think America has been true to her ideals?

A. I'm afraid to answer that, the Ku Klux Klan might give me a ducking.

Q. What is your idea of happiness?

A. Helpfulness.

Q. Who is your favorite hero in real life?

A. Eugene V. Debs. He dared to do what other men were afraid to do.

Q. Who is your favorite heroine in real life?

A. Kate O'Hare because she was willing to go to jail for her ideal of world peace and brotherhood.

Q. Do you think the voice of the people is heard at the polls?

A. No, I think money talks so loud that the voice of the people is drowned.

Q. What is the greatest obstacle to universal peace?

A. The human race.

Q. What is the slowest thing in the world?

A. Congress.

Q. Do you think that all political prisoners should be released?

A. Certainly. They opposed the World War on the ground that it was a commercial war. Now everyone with a grain of sense says it was. Their crime is they said it first.

Q. What is the matter with America?

A. Read *Babbitt* and you will find out.

Q. What is the outstanding deficiency of Americans?

A. Lack of originality. Everything is standardized, even our thoughts. The central motive of all our action is "What will others think about us?"

Q. What do you think of war?

A. Read John Dos Passos's *The Three Soldiers,* and you will know what I think of war, the most atrocious of human follies.

Q. Can you see any way out of our troubles?

A. Have you thought of divorce?

Q. Do you desire your sight more than anything else in the world?

A. No! No! I would rather walk with a friend in the dark than walk alone in the light.

Q. Which quality do you admire most in your teacher?

A. Her sense of humor; her many-sided sympathy; her passion for service.

Speech to Annual Convention
of Lions Clubs International

Cedar Point, Ohio, June 30, 1925

DEAR LIONS AND LADIES: I suppose you have heard the legend that represents opportunity as a capricious lady, who knocks at every door but once, and if the door isn't opened quickly, she passes on, never to return. And that is as it should be. Lovely, desirable ladies won't wait. You have to go out and grab 'em.

I am your opportunity. I am knocking at your door. I want to be adopted. The legend doesn't say what you are to do when several beautiful opportunities present themselves at the same door. I guess you have to choose the one you love best. I hope you will adopt me. I am the youngest here, and what I offer you is full of splendid opportunities for service.

The American Foundation for the Blind is only four years old. It grew out of the imperative needs of the blind, and was called into existence by the sightless themselves. It is national and international in scope and in importance. It represents the best and most enlightened thought on the subject that has been reached so far. Its object is to make the lives of the blind more worthwhile everywhere by increasing their economic value and giving them the joy of normal activity.

Try to imagine how you would feel if you were suddenly stricken blind today. Picture yourself stumbling and groping at noonday as in the night; your work, your independence, gone. In that dark world wouldn't you be glad if a friend took you by the hand and said, "Come with me and I will teach you how to do some of the things you used to do when you could see"? That is just the kind of friend the American Foundation is going to be to all the blind in this country if seeing people will give it the support it must have.

You have heard how through a little word dropped from the fingers of another, a ray of light from another soul touched the darkness of my mind and I found myself, found the world, found God. It is because my teacher learned about me and broke through the dark, silent imprisonment which held me that I am able to work for myself and for others. It is the caring we want more than money. The gift without the sympathy and interest of the giver is empty. If you care, if we can make the people of this great country care, the blind will indeed triumph over blindness.

The opportunity I bring to you, Lions, is this: To foster and sponsor the work of the American Foundation for the Blind. Will you not help me hasten the day when there shall be no preventable blindness; no little deaf children untaught; no blind man or woman unaided? I appeal to you Lions, you who have your sight, your hearing, you who are strong and brave and kind. Will you not constitute yourselves Knights of the Blind in this crusade against darkness?

I thank you.

Address to the Teachers
of the Deaf and of the Blind
Glasgow, Scotland, June 10, 1932

D EAR FRIENDS, As I stand before you in these glorious garments
[she had just been presented with a graduation robe] I feel like
Judith, who, before presenting herself at the tent of Holofernes,
arrayed herself in her richest attire—her bracelets, her earrings, her
necklaces, her fillet of purple, her pins of gold, and her jewelled rings. So
you have decked me out in splendour for the ceremony at the University
of Glasgow. Out of a very full heart I thank you.

Since I was eight years old I have been present and taken part in
many forms of exercises, and I want to say to you very sincerely this is
one of the most touching occasions I have ever attended. I could not
have received a more precious token of appreciation from the teachers
and friends of those whose limitations and difficulties I share. And it
makes me happy also to have Dr. and Mrs. Love here, so beautifully
linked with an event deeply significant in my life. For with you I hold in
affectionate regard one who has long been interested in the deaf especially, and generally in those whose handicaps multiply the difficulties
of life.

Your hands, dear Mrs. Love, have adorned me with bright feathers not
of my own plumage. But I will wear them as if they were mine, and hope
that in Scotland fine feathers will make me a fine bird.

The warm gratitude I feel for my own teacher makes me love all
teachers whose work is a staff of hope to the deaf and the blind. What
patience, what perseverance, what ingenuity are required to open a
child's mind, especially that of a handicapped child! When I look back
over the difficulties through which I have come, I marvel at the sustained effort that is exerted to combat the disorganizing, confusing, iso-
lating effects of deafness. And what shall I say of the skill and devotion of
those who open doors of opportunity for the sightless! When teachers
awaken the dormant faculties of a deaf or blind pupil, Prometheus-like
they must steal the fire of heaven, and with it put life into what is inert
and light up a darkness that has no end. Generations rise up and call
themselves blessed because they have lighted the lamp of thought in

many minds. When I consider how the deaf and the blind are led out of the house of bondage by the work of their teachers, I realize what shall some day happen to mankind when the highest education is attained.

Again, I thank you, dear friends.

Commencement Address
to Queen Margaret College
Glasgow, Scotland, June 15, 1932

Y OUNG WOMEN OF SCOTLAND, life is before you. Two voices are calling you. One comes from the marts of selfishness and force where success is won at any cost, and the other from the hilltops of justice and progress where even failure may ennoble. Two lights are in your horizon for you to choose. One is the fast-fading, will-o'-the-wisp of power and materialism, the other the slowly rising sun of human brotherhood. Two laws stand to-day opposed, each demanding your allegiance. One is the law of death which daily invents new means of combat; this law obliges the nations to be ever at war. The other is the law of peace, of labour, of salvation, which strives to deliver man from the scourges which assail him. One looks only for violent conquest, the other for the relief of suffering humanity. Two ways lie open before you, one leading to a lower and yet lower plane of life, where are heard the weeping of the poor, the cries of little children, and the moans of pain, where manhood and womanhood shrivel, and possessions destroy the possessor; and the other leading to the highlands of the mind where are heard the glad shouts of humanity, and honest effort is rewarded with immortality.

I have no doubt of your choice. Being the daughters of a heroic race, you will not shirk your responsibility. St. Margaret has shown you the way in which you must go. She is sending you out in the search not of things that you may own, but in the search for your true self, for your own way of thinking and serving, for the lives of other beings. You will seek to find what human life can be, and you will make the search with high courage and sober common sense. You will not reach the goal. Your life is stretched between the least that is left behind and the achievement still before you, of which every vision that we get seems only a glimmer of the truth that we shall some day win. Like your patron saint you will go forth to civilize, to enlighten, and to bless. Yes, you are going toward something great. I am on the way with you, and therefore I love you.

Address to the New Church
of Scotland (Swedenborgian)
Glasgow, Scotland, June 22, 1932

DEAR FRIENDS OF THE NEW CHURCH OF SCOTLAND, I greet you with the joy of spiritual kinship. It is good to be in this "green and pleasant land," and to find friends with whom I can unite in a happy community of faith. I cannot express better the sense of fellowship I experience here than by telling you what the writings of Emanuel Swedenborg have meant to me.

By giving me the golden key to the hidden treasures of the Bible he opened the gate of the Garden of Heaven for me, and showed me fair flowering paths where I love to walk. What precious herbs of healing grow there! What sweet smells of celestial flowers greet me! What thresholds of quiet I pass over, leaving behind me all the harsh, loud futilities of earth-life! There the Lamb of God walks whitely through the grass. In the Garden of the Lord sparkle countless rills and fountains. There the dews from Hermon fall upon my head. The trees, laden with golden fruit, murmur wisdom with their leaves, and the birds no longer sing wordless notes, but immortal truths. There blessed figures arrayed in light pass me and smile companionship with me; their beautiful hands guide me in paths of peace, and they whisper patience to me while I wait for my release unto greater service and a more satisfying self-expression.

There, with "The Divine Love and Wisdom" spiritually bright, I read words that give me eyes and thoughts that quicken my ear. As the air is made luminous by the sun, so the Word Ineffable makes bright all darkness.

Yes, the teachings of Emanuel Swedenborg have been my light and a staff in my hand, and by his vision splendid I am attended on my way.

Address in St. Bride's Parish Church

Bothwell, England, June 26, 1932

D EAR FRIENDS, I am always glad to bear witness to the blessing the Bible has been to me. Ever since I was a little girl I have read it constantly for courage and joy.

Through all kinds of difficulties the Bible has kept my hope of accomplishment bright. In the desert of darkness and silence the Bible has planted concepts of inward sight and hearing which have exercised an ever-increasing power over my thoughts. It has rendered less bitter the separation from those whom I have loved and lost a little while. It has made the spiritual world very real to me.

I should like to say to you, my friends, no matter what our creed or our interpretation of the Scriptures, that the Bible is our sure balance amid the confusion and wavering elements of earth-life. It gives us a right perspective of the great things God asks of us and the little things in which we waste our energies. It is a faithful reminder of our high capabilities, a fearless monitor against belittling aims. A daily walk in the sweet fields of the Word renews our faded enthusiasms and enlarges our aspirations. We have not learned the Lesson of Life if we do not every day open the Word for a moment of spiritual refreshment.

Address to the
National Institute for the Blind
London, England, July 4, 1932

SIR BEACHCROFT TOWSE AND FRIENDS, There could be no day more appropriate for the opening of the Massage School for the Blind than the 4th of July. To-day America is celebrating her independence, and to-day in London the blind and their friends are making another brave effort to secure the independence of the sightless. The spirit of independence is very strong in our race, and the hope of independence is the torch that lights the blind on their dark journey.

On this occasion it is encouraging to remember how far we have come since the days of degrading pity that banished the blind from the activities of human life to the by-ways of beggary and charity. To-day you are proclaiming, not by voice alone, but by deed, that you expect the blind to be in the vanguard of civilization. It is true that there is one problem modern civilization has solved. It might be summed up in the question, "Am I my brother's keeper?" The answer to this question is now definitely in the affirmative. Society has accepted responsibility for the unfortunate who, by reason of physical disability, are less fitted than their fellows to participate in the struggle for their maintenance. What we ask to-day of society is a larger independence for the handicapped.

How the thought smiles upon us, that the new massage school under the auspices of the National Institute for the Blind will house a high ideal of usefulness and independence for the sightless, and that your co-operation and goodwill are making this dream a bright reality! I do not forget that depression and widespread suffering have created demands that are endless and insistent. But we must brace ourselves for more and more self-denial. There is no "give" to the necessity of finding something to do for those who can work. I like to use myself as an example of what can be done for all the handicapped. If it was possible for one loving human being to enable me to find work and happiness despite triple limitation, how much easier it is to help those who are only blind!

Now, the new massage school is not a charity. Its friends ask your patronage for the students they are training, not because they are blind, but because they are intelligent, capable men and women. If you give them the right sort of help, they will become an asset to the community in which they live.

Please bear in mind, it is hard enough for those with all their faculties to succeed. The real problem of the sightless person begins when he seeks work. He cannot succeed alone. The world is made by the seeing and for the seeing. His education is comparatively easy, but teaching the world to move up on the bench of life and give him a chance to make good is not so easy.

I stand before you, myself deaf and blind, and with halting speech I plead with you to do unto my blind fellows as you would have others do unto you. Remember, blind people are just like other people in the dark. They have the same ambitions and feelings you have. They want the same things you do. They want work, useful work and some of life's sweet satisfactions. When the public adopts an attitude of understanding and helpfulness, the difficulties of the sightless will no longer be insurmountable. Through you they will triumph over blindness. Only then will God's Commandment be obeyed, "Put not a stumbling-block in the way of the blind, nor make life bitter for the deaf."

These are times that try men's souls, but we must not shrink from facing the crisis with open eyes and courageous minds. If we stand fast now, posterity will thank us for our constancy.

Depression and selfishness are not easily conquered, but conquer them we must if civilization is to advance. What we may obtain with little effort we esteem too lightly. It is struggle only that gives victory its preciousness. Men are not honoured for the difficulties that beset their lives, but for the overcoming of them.

If people everywhere would only minimize their differences and think of the fine qualities that unite them, they would strive to bring order and unity out of the discords created by fear and strife. True patriotism now is to unite in casting our weight on the side of all work that liberates, enlightens, and turns disaster into a bridge-road to a nobler civilization.

Address to the
National Council of Women

London, England, July 7, 1932

M RS. FRANKLIN AND FRIENDS, I am proud to be one of this gathering of the National Council of Women. I wish to express my interest in everything that concerns women.

I believe that women have it in their power to make civilization minister to the comfort and happiness of all. But before we can accomplish this, we must understand the world we live in, physical and spiritual. By the physical I mean our environment and how to control it. By the spiritual I mean an intelligent study of economics, industry, and politics. What we need to learn is how to use wealth for progressive education, for public hygiene, for decrease of crime, delinquency, and injustice, for art, beauty, and human happiness.

Furthermore, I believe women can make the world safe from war, and it is incumbent upon them to use this power before it is too late. We must learn to think down every wall that divides us from our fellow-creatures and prevents us from giving them sympathy and help. Wholeheartedly I join hands with all who, like the National Council of Women, go forth to liberate, to enlighten and to bless. Always in my dreams I hear the turn of the key that shall close for ever the brazen gates of war, and the fall of the last rampart that stands between humanity and a happier world.

Speech to Knights of the Blind

Chicago, Illinois, 1953

DEAR LIONS, my Knights of the Blind, as I have always called you. What a wonderful moment this is, as I stand before you and think of the light you are spreading among the peoples of the world. As I travel from state to state and country to country, I catch you Lions hunting vigorously for means to further this noble purpose. Recently I traveled in Central and South America, trying to get data concerning the blind. I was privileged to meet the Lions in Lima and Panama. I had known that the Lions of the United States had chosen as their basic activity work for the blind, but I had not realized that they had leaped over the walls of different languages to unite in their service to the captives of the dark.

During my journey, I learned that over a half million blind persons live south of the United States and, to my dismay, I found that just a pitifully small number had friends who were able to lead them along the dark roads. Throughout Latin America the blind are trying desperately to get an education, and their only equipment is Braille hand slates. They must have Braille printing presses if the accumulated treasures of literature, science and philosophy are to enrich their sightless lives.

About 18 months ago, an historic conference was held in Montevideo by experts, many of them blind, where Spanish and Portuguese is spoken. The technical and linguistic difficulties were overcome and since then the American Foundation for Overseas Blind and the Kellog Foundation have cooperated and installed a model Braille press in Mexico. The two foundations have also installed similar equipment in Recife for the publication of books in Portuguese. But many of the blind are still crying out for books to develop their minds and widen their opportunities.

I am encouraged to suggest that you Lions of all the Americas combine to supply them with Braille printing equipment. If this idea pleases you, perhaps you Lions from the United States and you Lions from Latin America can include among your many projects the raising of funds for a Braille press to be established in a carefully selected area, from which embossed books can go to the blind of other regions. Certainly, dear

Lions, it would gratify me inexpressibly if through your bounty the blind of all Latin America might draw freely from the waters of literature to satisfy their cravings of the mind and the spirit.

I thank you.

Keller at 45 years old. She spoke in public for almost eighty years.

Chronology of Selected Major Speeches

Speech at Andover, Andover, Massachusetts, May 1891

Address of Helen Keller at Mt. Airy, Philadelphia, Pennsylvania, Pennsylvania, July 8, 1896

Our Duties to the Blind, Boston, Massachusetts, January 5, 1904

The Heaviest Burden of the Blind, New York City, January 15, 1907

The Plain Truth, Boston, Massachusetts, August 27, 1907

The Conservation of Eyesight, Boston, Massachusetts, February 14, 1911

The Education of the Blind, Boston, Massachusetts, August 16, 1912

The Heart and the Hand or the Right Use of Our Senses, Boston, Massachusetts, March 24, 1913

The Gift of Speech, New York City, April 8, 1913

A New Light Is Coming, Sagamore Beach, Massachusetts, July 8, 1913

Menace of the Militarist Program, New York City, December 19, 1915

Strike Against War, New York City, January 5, 1916

Why I Became an IWW, New York City, January 1918

Onward, Comrades!, New York City, December 31, 1920

The Vaudeville Circuit, Throughout the United States, 1919–24

Speech to Annual Convention of Lions Clubs International, Cedar Point, Ohio, June 30, 1925

Address to the Teachers of the Deaf and of the Blind, Glasgow, Scotland, June 10, 1932

Commencement Address to Queen Margaret College, Glasgow, Scotland, June 15, 1932

Address to the New Church of Scotland (Swedenborgian), Glasgow, Scotland, June 22, 1932

Address in St. Bride's Parish Church, Bothwell, England, June 26, 1932

Address to the National Institute for the Blind, London, England, July 4, 1932

Address to the National Council of Women, London, England, July 7, 1932

Address to the Rotarians of Inverness, Scotland, September 8, 1932

Speech to Knights of the Blind, Chicago, Illinois, 1953

Notes

Foreword

1. Kenneth Burke, *Language as Symbolic Action: Essays in Life, Literature, and Method* (Berkeley: University of California Press, 1966), p. 10.

Introduction

1. Other well-known blind and deaf people who lived at the same time as Keller include Laura Bridgman, Edith Thomas, Willie Elizabeth Robin, Tommy Stringer, Breta Cornelius, Marion Duffin, Joan Higgens, Leonard Dowdy, Jackie Coker, Richard Kinney, Helen Siefert, Helen May Martin, and Kathryne Mary Prick. The research is reported in Marguerita Mooers Marshall, "The Woman of It," *The Evening World* (4 August 1930).

2. Lash, Joseph P., *Helen and Teacher: The Story of Helen Keller and Anne Sullivan Macy* (New York: Delacorte Press, 1980); Fillippeli, Susan E., "The Revolutionary Rhetoric of Helen Keller." M.A. Thesis, University of Georgia, 1985; Nelson, Nancy J., "A Critical Analysis of Helen Keller's Socialist Speaking." M.A. Thesis, South Dakota, 1984; and Klages, Mary Krag, "More Wonderful Than Fiction: The Representation of Helen Keller." Ph.D. dissertation, Stanford University, 1989.

3. For a fuller discussion of the case of Tommy Stringer, see the *Sixtieth Annual Report of the Trustees of the Perkins Institution and Massachusetts School for the Blind for the Year Ending September 30, 1891*, Boston: Wright & Potter Printing Co., 1892, pp. 236–98. The speech text comes from pp. 291–92.

4. The speech text comes from *Lions Clubs International NEWS*, a newsletter published by the organization. The national office of Lions Clubs International in Oak Brook, Illinois sent me my copy.

5. The Helen Keller Archives of the American Foundation for the Blind in New York City is currently not in operation due to financial problems.

Chapter One

1. Keller, *World*, pp. 113–14; Keller, *World*, p. 116, Keller, *Teacher*, p. 8.
2. See Keller, *Story*, p. 30; and Keller, *Story*, p. 35.
3. Keller, *Story*, p. 33.
4. Keller, *My Religion* (Garden City, NY: Doubleday Page & Co., 1927), pp. 29–30.

5. Keller, *Story*, pp. 36–37; Keller, *Religion*, p. 153; Keller, *World*, pp. 113–21.

6. Walker Percy, "The Delta Factor," *The Message in the Bottle* (New York: Farrar, 1954), p. 35.

7. Keller, *Teacher*, pp. 41–43.

8. Keller, *Story*, pp. 43–45.

9. Keller, *Teacher*, p. 61.

10. Keller, *Story*, p. 78.

11. Keller, *American Annals of the Deaf* (1913) in *Gallaudet Encyclopedia of Deaf People and Deafness*, ed. John V. Van Cleve, vol. 2 (New York: McGraw-Hill Book Company, Inc., 1987), p. 125.

12. Keller, *Teacher*, p. 62

13. Keller, *Story*, p. 81; Keller, *Teacher*, p. 63.

14. Keller, *Story*, p. 37.

15. Keller, *My Key of Life*, pp. 3–4; Keller, *Out of the Dark*, p. 108; Keller, *Story*, p. 128.

16. Keller, *Story*, p. 143.

17. Lash, p. 181.

18. Merton S. Keith, "Final Preparation for College." *Helen Keller Souvenir No. 2 1892–1899.* Washington, D. C.: Volta Bureau, 1899, pp. 37n.

19. Sullivan, in Keller, *Story*, pp. 372–73.

20. Lash, p. 212; Lash, p. 62. The term "Schoolhouse Earth" comes from a "Family Circus" comic, June 15, 1994.

21. Keller, *Story*, p. 48.

22. Keller, "The Hand of the World," in Foner, p. 42.

Chapter Two

1. Helen Keller, "A Chant of Darkness," in *The World I Live In*, p. 194.

2. Helen Keller, *The Story of My Life*, pp. 229 and 231.

3. Lash, p. 101; Anne Sullivan in 60th Annual Report, Perkins, p. 108; and Michael Anagnos, 57th Annual Report, Perkins.

4. Helen Keller, *Teacher*, p. 118 and Lash, p. 284.

5. Helen Keller, *World*, pp. 84–85.

6. Helen Keller, "How I Became a Socialist," in Foner, p. 26; Helen Keller, "The Unemployed," in Foner, p. 36; Helen Keller, "The Hand of the World," in Foner, p. 42.

7. Helen Keller, "The Hand of the World," in Foner, pp. 43, 42–43, and 44.

8. Helen Keller, "Hand of the World," in Foner, p. 41; Helen Keller, "The Menace of the Militarist Program," in Foner, pp. 73–74; and Helen Keller, "The Menace of the Militarist Program," in Foner, p. 73.

9. Helen Keller, "How I Became a Socialist," in Foner, p. 25; Helen Keller, "Introduction to *Arrows in the Gale: Poems by Arturo Giovannitti*, in Foner, p. 58; and Helen Keller, "A New Light Is Coming."

10. Helen Keller, "New Vision for the Blind," in Foner, p. 56; Helen Keller, "What Is the IWW?" in Foner, p. 91.

11. Helen Keller, "Why I Became an IWW," in Foner, p. 84.

12. Fillippeli, p. 120.

13. Michael Osborn, "Archetypal Metaphor in Rhetoric: The Light-Dark Family," *Quarterly Journal of Speech* 53 (1967): 115–26, especially p. 117; Michael Osborn, "The Evolution of the Archetypal Sea in Rhetoric and Poetic," *The Quarterly Journal of Speech* 63 (1977): 351–63; and Michael Osborn and Douglas Ehninger, "The Metaphor in Public Address," *Speech Monographs* 29 (1962): 223–34.

14. Osborn, "Archetypal," pp. 117 and 120.

15. Osborn, "Archetypal," p. 118.

16. Helen Keller, *Story*, p. 35.

17. W. H. Auden, *The Enchanted Flood: The Romantic Iconography of the Sea* (New York: Random House, 1950), p. 27, quoted in Osborn, "The Evolution," p. 356.

18. Helen Keller, "To the Strikers at Little Falls, New York," in Foner, p. 37.

19. Helen Keller, letter to Dr. Frederick Tilney (8 February 1928), in "A Comparative Sensory Analysis of Helen Keller and Laura Bridgman II: Its Bearing on the Future Development of the Human Brain," by Frederick Tilney, M.D., *Archives of Neurology and Psychiatry* 21 (1929): 1242.

20. Dhyani Ywahoo, *Voices of Our Ancestors: Cherokee Teachings from the Wisdom Fire* (Boston: Shambhala, 1987), p. 118.

21. Carroll C. Arnold, *Criticism of Oral Rhetoric* (Columbus, OH: Bell and Howell Company, 1974), pp. 168–69.

22. Helen Keller, *Helen Keller in Scotland: A Personal Record Written by Herself* (London: Methuen and Co., Ltd., 1933), pp. 205–6.

23. Helen Keller, *Story*, pp. 136–37.

Chapter Three

1. Keller, *Story*, p. 55; Nella Braddy Henney, "Introduction" to *Teacher*, by Keller, pp. 12–13.

2. Braddy, p. 201; Braddy, pp. 201–2, Lash, p. 393.

3. Some tests showed that Keller's sense of smell was, perhaps, a bit better than that of "normal" people.

4. Fillippeli, p. 62; Helen Keller, *Out of the Dark: Essays, Letters, and Addresses on Physical and Social Vision* (Garden City, NY: Doubleday, Page & Company, 1914), pp. 21–22.

5. Keller, *Out of the Dark*, pp. 22–23; Letter of S. Stanwood Menken to Major Moses Miguel, in Lash, p. 555.

6. Fillippeli, p. 106.

7. "Miss Sullivan's Methods," anon. ts. Perkins Archives, in Lash, pp. 144–45.

8. Lash, pp. 132–33.

9. *Annual Report of the Perkins Institution*, 1847, p. 35 and pp. 11–12.

10. William Jolly, *Education: Its Principles and Practice as Developed by George Combe* (London: Macmillan and Company, 1879), pp. 443–44 and p. 444.

11. Mary Krag Klages, "More Wonderful Than Any Fiction: The Representation of Helen Keller," diss., Stanford University, 1989, pp. 180–81.

12. Thomas D. Cutsforth, *The Blind in School and Society: A Psychological Study* (New York: American Foundation for the Blind, 1951), pp. 51, 48–49, 55,

and 56; Pierre Villey, *The World of the Blind* (New York: 1930), quoted in Lash, p. 600.

13. Cutsforth, p. 62; Cutsforth, quoted in Lash, p. 607; Lash, p. 608.

14. Keller, *Midstream*, pp. 12 and 13.

15. Keller, *Midstream*, p. xix.

16. Keller, *World*, pp. xi–xii; Keller, "Sense and Sensibility," *Century Magazine* (Feb. 1908): 566.

17. Keller, in Foner, p. 75; Keller, in Foner, p. 113.

18. Keller, in Foner, p. 26.

19. Keller, "Sense and Sensibility," p. 566 or Keller, *World*, p. 40. Keller frequently repeated passages in different speeches and/or books and essays. Where multiple sources exist, I try to note them using "or."

20. Keller, "Sense and Sensibility: Part II," p. 782 or Keller, *World*, pp. 127–28; Keller, *World*, p. 40.

21. Keller, *World*, pp. 123–25; Keller, *World*, p. 124.

22. Keller, "Sense and Sensibility, Part II," p. 773 or Keller, *World*, p. 89.

23. Keller, *World*, pp. 104–5 or "Sense and Sensibility, Part II," p. 777.

24. Keller, *Story of My Life*, pp. 88–89; *Annual Report of the Perkins Institution*, 1891, p. 72.

25. John Albert Macy, "Helen Keller's Critics," *Boston Evening Transcript* (27 May 1903): n. pag.

26. Lash, p. 362; Keller, *Midstream*, p. 166 and pp. 164–65; Keller, *The Open Door*, p. 25.

27. Keller, *The Open Door*, p. 25 or *World*, p. 83; Keller, *World*, pp. 80–81. Keller quoted Diderot in French and gave the English translation in a footnote.

28. Keller, *World*, p. 28; Keller, *Out of the Dark*, pp. 3–17 or Keller, *World*, pp. 28–37 and p. 37.

29. Keller, *Midstream*, p. 259.

30. Keller, "Sense and Sensibility," p. 576 or *World*, p. 80; Keller, *World*, p. 84.

31. Keller, *Midstream*, p. xvii; Keller, *World*, p. 10 and p. 8.

32. Keller, *Story* p. 53.

33. Keller, "Sense and Sensibility: Part II," p. 777 or *World*, p. 108.

34. I. A. Richards, *The Philosophy of Rhetoric* (New York: Oxford University Press, 1965, especially pp. 87–138. The quotations are from pp. 131 and 94. For an historical perspective of the treatment of metaphor, see Max Black, *Models and Metaphors: Studies in Language and Philosophy* (Ithaca, NY: Cornell University Press, 1962), pp. 25–47.

35. Keller, "Sense and Sensibility," p. 774; Keller, *My Key of Life*, p. 15.

36. Keller, *Let Us Have Faith*, p. 4.

37. Keller, *My Religion*, last page.

38. Keller, *Story*, p. 148.

39. Keller, "Sense and Sensibility: Part II," p. 774 or *World*, pp. 89–90.

40. Keller, *My Religion*, pp. 38, 38–39, and 39.

41. Emmanuel Swedenborg, *Heaven and Hell*, quoted in Keller, *My Religion*, pp. 46–47

42. See John Elliott Braun, "The Philosophical Roots of the Nineteenth Century 'Repose' of Rhetoric, with Emphasis on the Idea of Communication

in the Thought of Josiah Royce." Ann Arbor, Michigan: University of Michigan, 1977.

43. Ernst Cassirer, *Essay on Man: An Introduction to a Philosophy of Human Culture* (New Haven, CT: Yale University Press, 1944); Josiah Royce, *The Spirit of Modern Philosophy* (Boston: Houghton, Mifflin and Company, 1897); George Berkeley, *The Teaching of George Berkeley, Bishop of Cloyne*, ed. A. A. Luce and T. E. Jessop, 9 vols. (London: 1948); Immanuel Kant, *Critique of Pure Reason*, 1781; and Frederick Copleston, S. J., *A History of Philosophy*, vol. 5 (Hobbes to Hume) (Westminster, MD: The Newman Press, 1959), especially pp. 202–59; Keller, *Midstream*, p. 12; Keller, *My Key of Life*, pp. 13–14.

44. Dr. James Kerr Love, "The Childhood of Helen Keller," *The Teacher of the Deaf* (Feb. 1933), in Lash, p. 611; Keller, *World*, p. 151; Keller, *Story*, p. 20.

45. Keller, *Story*, p. 19.

46. Fillippeli, pp. 96–97; Keller, *World*, pp. 84–85.

47. Lash, p. 463; Fillippeli, p. 118.

Chapter Four

1. Keller discussed the complimentary labels in her letter to Senator Robert M. La Follette, August 1924, in Foner, p. 113.

2. The information on Lions Clubs International comes from "Lions Clubs International Fact Sheet," published by the organization's national office in Oak Brook, Illinois.

A mature Keller still reading. She always liked to speak, read, and write. She wrote several books and essays, and others wrote many books and articles about her.

Selected Bibliography on Helen Keller

Archival Materials

The American Foundation for the Blind, New York City
Helen Keller Birthplace, Tuscumbia, Alabama
Helen Keller Eye Research Foundation, Birmingham, Alabama
Lions Club International, Oak Brook, Illinois
National Federation of the Blind, Baltimore, Maryland
National Library Service for the Blind and Physically Handicapped, Library of
  Congress, Washington, D.C.
Samuel P. Hayes Library, Perkins School for the Blind, Watertown, Massachusetts
Schlesinger Library (Ratliffe College), Cambridge, Massachusetts
Swedenborg Foundation, New York City
Volta Bureau (also known as the Alexander Graham Bell Association for the
  Deaf), Washington, D.C.

Books and Articles By Helen Keller

Below is a complete list of writings in English by Helen Keller:

Keller, Helen Adams. "Address to the Blind of New York City." *Outlook for the
  Blind* 7 (1914): 91–92.
_____. "Albert Einstein." *Home Magazine* 3, no. 4 (1931): 6, 129.
_____. "All Weather Is Good Weather." *Home Magazine* 9, no. 3 (1934): 12.
_____. "An Apology for Going to College." *McClure's Magazine* 25 (June 1905):
  190–96.
_____. "An Appeal to Reason." *Appeal to Reason* (December 1910).
_____. "Are We Wasters of Time?" *Home Magazine* 7, no. 1 (1933): 6.
_____. "The Beauty of Silence." *Home Magazine* 11, no. 5 (1935): 8.
_____. "Blazing the Trail." *Home Magazine* 10, no. 4 (1934): 8.
_____. "Blind Leaders." *Outlook for the Blind* 32 (1913): 231–36.
_____. "Birth Control." New York *Call* (26 November 1915).
_____. "Brutal Treatment of the Unemployed in Sacramento." Sacramento (Cal-
  ifornia) *Star* (16 March 1914).
_____. "A Call for Harmony." New York *Call* (4 January 1913).
_____. "A Chant of Darkness." *Century Magazine* 76 (1908): 142–47.
_____. "Chat About the Hand." *Century Magazine* 69 (1905): 454–65.
_____. "A Christmas Challenge." *Home Magazine* 2, no. 6 (1930): 8.
_____. "Christmas Day Is Children's Day." *Home Magazine* 6 (1931): 8.
_____. "Christmas in the Dark." *The Ladies Home Journal* (December 1906).

_____. "A Christmas Thought." *Home Magazine* 6, no. 6 (1932): 6, 87.

_____. "The Christmas Vision." *Home Magazine* 8, no. 6 (1933): 12, 71.

_____. "The Common Good Is an Ideal Which Is Mightier Than Any Man and Worthy of All Men." *Home Magazine* 10, no. 5 (1934): 13.

_____. "The Correct Training of a Blind Child." *Ladies Home Journal* 25, no. 5 (1905): 12, 76.

_____. "Crushing Out Our Children's Lives." *Home Magazine* 4, no. 2 (1931): 10.

_____. "Deeds of Immortality." *Home Magazine* 11, no. 6 (1935): 9.

_____. "Do Most Men Know the Color of Their Wives' Eyes?" *Literary Digest* 115, no. 9 (1933): 35–36.

_____. "Dreams That Come True." *Personality* (December 1927): 67–74. Also in *The Helper* 81, no. 1 (1927): 2–14.

_____. "The Earth Is Still in the Making." *Home Magazine* 6, no. 3 (1932): 6.

_____. "Easter." *Home Magazine* 5, no. 4 (1932): 6.

_____. "Easter Message." *Home Magazine* 9, no. 4 (1934): 6.

_____. *Edith and the Bees. Skinner. The Emerald Story Book.* New York: Duffield & Co., 1915, pp. 226–29.

_____. "End the Blockade of Soviet Russia." New York *Call* (10 November 1919).

_____. "The England That Helen Keller Sees," *New York Times Magazine* (10 July 1932): 7.

_____. "An Enigma." *Mentor* 2 (1892): 13–16.

_____. *The Faith of Helen Keller: The Life of a Great Woman, with Selections from Her Writings.* Edited by Jack Belck. Kansas City, MO: Hallmark Cards, Inc., 1967.

_____. "The Flaw in Shaw." *Reader's Digest* 23, no. 133 (1933): 101–3.

_____. "The Ford Peace Plan Is Doomed to Failure." New York *Call* (16 December 1915).

_____. "From the Woman Warrior." In *The Norton Book of Women's Lives.* By Phyllis Ross. New York: W. W. Norton, 1993.

_____. "The Frost King." *Mentor* 2 (1892): 13–16.

_____. "The Goddess Who Knows Not Pity." *Home Magazine* 6, no. 2 (1932): 6.

_____. "Going Back to School: The True Meaning of the Value of Education." *Home Magazine* 10, no. 3 (1934): 6.

_____. "Great American Women: The Heroic Careers of Three Famous Champions of Women's Rights." *Home Magazine* 5, no. 2 (1932): 8, 113.

_____. "The Great Choice." *Home Magazine* 5, no. 1 (1932): 8.

_____. "The Great Day." *Golden Book Magazine* 20, no. 115 (1934): 39–40.

_____. "The Greatness of God Is Expressed in Trees." *Home Magazine* 8, no. 2 (1933): 8, 91.

_____. "The Hand of the World." *American Magazine* (December 1912): 43–45. Reprinted in part in "The Hand of the World by Helen Keller, the Blind Girl Who Overcame Great Difficulties." *Appeal to Reason Leaflets*, No. 6. Girard, KS: Appeal to Reason.

_____. "He Helped People to See: The Story of Clarence Hawkes." *Psychology* 15, no. 1 (1930): 31–32, 72.

_____. "The Heaviest Burden of the Blind." *Outlook for the Blind* 1 (1907): 10–12.

_____. "Helen Keller at Wrentham." In *No Walls of Stone: An Anthology of Literature by Deaf and Hard of Hearing Writers*. Washington, D.C.: Gallaudet University Press, 1992.

_____. "Helen Keller Explains How She Unknowingly Plagiarized." New York *Herald* (29 March 1903).

_____. *Helen Keller: Her Socialist Years*. Edited by Philip S. Foner. New York: International Publishers, 1967.

_____. *Helen Keller in Scotland: A Personal Record Written by Herself*. Edited by James Kerr Love. London: Methuen & Co., Ltd., 1933.

_____. "Helen Keller on 'Sense and Sensibility.'" *Association Review* 10 (1908): 186–90.

_____. *Helen Keller Souvenirs*. First and Second Editions. Washington, D.C.: Volta Bureau, 1891 and 1899.

_____. *Helen Keller Under the Southern Cross*. Part II. Cape Town, South Africa: Juta & Co., Ltd., 1952.

_____. *Helen Keller's Journal, 1936–1937*. Garden City, NY: Doubleday and Company, Inc., 1938.

_____. "Helen Keller's Letter to the Convention." *AAWB* (1909): 90–91.

_____. "Help Soviet Russia." *The Toiler* (19 November 1921).

_____. "Heroism." *Home Magazine* 8, no. 3 (1933): 6, 75.

_____. "Holiday in England." *Outlook for the Blind* 24 (1930): 14–16.

_____. "Honoring One We Love." *AAWB* (1927): 157–58.

_____. "How I Became a Socialist." New York *Call* (3 November 1912).

_____. *How I Would Help the World*. Rancho Palos Verdes, CA: Wayfarers Chapel, 1984.

_____. "How the Blind May Be Helped." *Putnam's Monthly* (April 1907): 70–72.

_____. "How to Become a Writer: A Letter to a Blind Boy." *World's Work* 19 (April, 1910): 12765–66.

_____. "How to Work Up a Panic." In *The Week-End Library: Issue of 1930*. Garden City, NY: Doubleday, 1930.

_____. "I Am Blind—Yet I See. I Am Deaf—Yet I Hear." *American Magazine* 107, no. 6 (1929): 44, 152–56.

_____. "I Must Speak: A Plea to the American Woman." *Ladies Home Journal* 26, no. 2 (1909).

_____. "If Women Dared to Do." *Home Magazine* 1, no. 4 (1930): 9.

_____. "If You Have Friends You Can Endure Anything." *American Magazine* (September 1929).

_____. "Immortality." *Home Magazine* 8, no. 4 (1933): 8.

_____. "The Importance of Reading." *Home Magazine* 2, no. 4 (1930): 6, 106.

_____. "In Behalf of the IWW." *The Liberator* (March 1918).

_____. "In Defense of Fred Warren." New York *Call* (1 January 1911).

_____. "Independence Day." *Home Magazine* 10, no. 1 (1934): 6.

_____. "Intelligent Reading." *Home Magazine* 8, no. 1 (1933): 6.

_____. "Introduction." *Arrows in the Gale*. By Arturo Giovannitti. Riverside, CT: Hillacre Book House, 1914.

_____. "Introduction." *The True Christian Religion*. New York: E. P. Dutton & Co., 1933.

_____. "Is Marriage the Highest Fulfillment of a Girl's Life?" *Home Magazine* 2, no. 5 (1930): 6, 129.

_____. "John Hitz as I Knew Him." *Outlook for the Blind* (July 1908).

_____. "June Skies." *Home Magazine* 5, no. 6 (1932): 6, 77.

_____. "A King at My Fingertips." *Good Housekeeping* 94 (1932): 28–29, 176–77.

_____. "Knights of the Blind." *The Lion* 10, no. 5 (1927): 11, 34.

_____. "Know Thyself." *Home Magazine* 2, no. 3 (1930): 6 and 117.

_____. *Lend a Hand* (March 1988): 137–46.

_____. "Let Us Create Beauty." *Home Magazine* 5, no. 3 (1932): 6.

_____. *Let Us Have Faith.* Garden City, NY: Doubleday Doran, and Company, 1941.

_____. "Letter of Helen A. Keller." *American Annals of the Deaf* 44, No. 2 (1899): 138–39.

_____. "Letter on the Endowment Fund of the American Foundation for the Blind." *Outlook for the Blind* 21, no. 4 (1928): 34–35.

_____. "A Letter to Mark Twain." Read by Mark Twain, New York Association for the Blind meeting, 29 March 1906.

_____. Letter to *North Alabamian*, reprinted in *Our Mountain Home*, 9 November 1891.

_____. "The Light of Faith" (reel). New York: Swedenborg Foundation, 1980.

_____. "Love Ye One Another." *Home Magazine* 3, no. 5 (1931): 6, 115.

_____. "Magic in Your Fingers." *Home Magazine* 5, no. 5 (1932): 8, 90.

_____. "Making a Happy Home." *Home Magazine* 7, no. 6 (1933): 6.

_____. "Mark Twain as Revealed by Himself to Helen Keller." *American Magazine* (August 1929).

_____. "Marks." *Home Magazine* 2, no. 1 (1930): 6.

_____. "Menace of the Militarist Program." New York *Call* (20 December 1915).

_____. *Midstream: My Later Life.* Garden City, NY: Doubleday, Doran & Co., 1929.

_____. *The Miracle of a Life: The Autobiography of Helen Keller.* New York: Hodder and Stoughton, 1909.

_____. "Miss Keller's Speech of Presentation." *Outlook for the Blind* 21, no. 2 (1927): 12–13.

_____. "The Modern Girl." *Home Magazine* 1, no. 6 (1930): 6.

_____. "The Modern Woman." *The Metropolitan Magazine* 37, no. 2 (December 1912): 22–23, 57.

_____. "The Mother's Mission." *Home Magazine* 4, no. 4 (1931): 12, 93.

_____. "My Animal Friends." *Zoological Society Bulletin* 26, no. 5 (1923): 111–18.

_____. "My Dreams." *Century Magazine* 77 (1908): 69–74.

_____. "My Future as I See It." *Ladies Home Journal* 20, no. 12 (November 1903): 11.

_____. *My Key of Life.* New York: T. Y. Crowell Co., 1926 (same as *Optimism*).

_____. "My Message to You." *Child Life* (April 1931).

_____. *My Religion.* Garden City, NY: Doubleday Page & Co., 1927.

_____. "My Story." *The Youth's Companion* (4 January 1894).

_____. "Nature's Storehouse of Health, Pays a Yearly Bonus of Happiness." *Good Housekeeping* (January 1933): 38–39, 140–42.

_____. "A Neglected Treasure." *Home Magazine* 9, no. 6 (1934): 6.

_____. "A New Chime for the Christmas Bells." *The Metropolitan Magazine* (January 1913).

_____. "A New Light Is Coming." New York *Call* (8 July 1913).

_____. "New Vision for the Blind." *Justice* (25 October 1913).

_____. "The New Woman's Party." New York *Call* (9 June 1916).

_____. *The New York That Helen Keller "Sees."* 1932. p. 8.

_____. "Noise." *Home Magazine* 4 (1931): 8.

_____. "O! Brave New World That Has Such People in It." *Red Cross Magazine* 14, no. 9 (1919): 31–35, 73–74.

_____. "An Occupation for the Deaf." Presented at the International Congress on the Education of the Deaf, West Trenton, 18–23 June 1933. Printed by students of the New Jersey School for the Deaf.

_____. "On Her Deprivations." *New Outlook for the Blind* 62 (September 1968): 220.

_____. "The Only Kind of War I Believe In." *The New Leader* (25 July 1925).

_____. "Onward, Comrades!" New York *Call* (30 January 1921).

_____. *The Open Door.* Garden City, NY: Doubleday and Company, Inc., 1957.

_____. *Optimism, an Essay.* New York: T. Y. Cromwell Co., 1903 (same as *My Key of Life*).

_____. "Our Coming Great Adventure." *Home Magazine* 12, no. 2 (1935): 40.

_____. "Our Duties to the Blind." Paper presented at the First Annual Meeting of the Massachusetts Association for Promoting the Interests of the Adult Blind, Boston, Perkins Hall, 5 January 1904.

_____. *Out of the Dark: Essays, Letters, and Addresses on Physical and Social Vision.* Garden City, NY: Doubleday, Page and Company, 1913.

_____. *Peace at Eventide.* London: Methuen and Co., Ltd., 1932.

_____. "A Plea for Recognition of Soviet Russia." New York *Call* (27 February 1921).

_____. *The Practice of Optimism.* London: Hadder and Stoughton, 1909.

_____. "Preventable Blindness." *Ladies Home Journal* (January 1907).

_____. "Prevention of Blindness and Conservation of Eyesight." Presented at the Massachusetts Association for Promoting the Interests of the Blind, Boston, 14 February 1911.

_____. "Put Your Husband in the Kitchen." *Atlantic Monthly* 150, no. 2 (1932): 140–47.

_____. "The Rand School." New York *Call* (30 December 1922).

_____. "Reading by Helen Keller from a Poem by Henry W. Longfellow," presented at the Commencement Exercises of the Perkins Institution for the Blind, Boston, 6 June 1893.

_____. "Rejoice with Spring." *Home Magazine* 7, no. 4 (1933): 8.

_____. "The Seeing Eye: A Few Words of Kindly Praise for This New Dog Service By One Who Can Well Understand Its True Worth." *Home Magazine* 12, no. 3 (1935): 16.

_____. "The Seeing Hand." *Victorian Readers*, seventh book, 1930: 176–77.

_____. "Seek the Cause." *Home Magazine* 7, no. 3 (1933): 6.

_____. "Sense and Sensibility: Part I." *Century Magazine* 75 (February 1908): 566–77.

_____. "Sense and Sensibility: Part II." *Century Magazine* 75 (March 1908): 773–83.

_____. "The Simplest Way to Be Happy." *Home Magazine* 7, no. 2 (1933): 6.

_____. "Sister Mabel." *St. Nicholas* (August 1890): 892.

_____. "Social Causes of Blindness." New York *Call* (15 February 1911).

_____. "Something to Think About." *Home Magazine* 2, no. 2 (1930): 13, 116.

_____. "The Song of the Stone Wall." *Century Magazine* 79 (1909): 215–25.

_____. *The Song of the Stone Wall.* New York: The Century Co., 1910.

_____. "Spirit of Easter." *The Youth's Companion* 78, no. 13 (1904).

_____. "The Story of Helen Keller Told by Herself." *The Youth's Companion* (1895): 3–15.

_____. "The Story of My Life." *Ladies Home Journal* 19, nos. 5–10 (1902).

_____. *The Story of My Life.* New York: Grosset & Dunlap, 1911.

_____. *The Story of My Life.* New York: Lancer Books, Inc., 1968.

_____. *The Story of My Life.* Adapted by C. N. Douglas. Illustrated by A. deZuniga. West Haven, CT: Pendulum Press, Inc., 1974.

_____. *The Story of My Life: New School Edition with Teachings and Study Helps.* Boston: Houghton Mifflin Co., 1928.

_____. "Strike Against War." New York *Call* (6 January 1916).

_____. "Summer Day in Scotland." *Home Magazine* 10, no. 2 (1934): 50.

_____. *Teacher: Anne Sullivan Macy; a Tribute by the Foster-Child of Her Mind.* Introduction by Nella Brady Henney. New York: Doubleday and Company, Inc., 1955.

_____. "A Thanksgiving Prayer." *Home Magazine* 6, no. 6 (1932): 6.

_____. "Thanksgiving Thoughts." *Home Magazine* 8, no. 5 (1933): 8.

_____. "A Thought for the New Year." *Home Magazine* 3, no. 1 (1931): 17.

_____. "Three Days to See." *Atlantic Monthly* 151, no. 1 (1933): 35–42.

_____. "Three Days to See: Condensed from the *Atlantic Monthly.*" *Reader's Digest* 22, no. 131 (1933): 1–4.

_____. "To an English Woman-Suffragist." Manchester (England) *Advertiser* (3 March 1911). Reprinted in part in the New York *Call* (14 May 1911).

_____. "To Eugene V. Debs." New York *Call* (24 April 1919). Also in *Appeal to Reason* (17 May 1919).

_____. "To Morris Hillquit." New York *Call* (5 November 1917).

_____. "To the Editor of the New York *Evening Sun.*" New York *Sun* (8 June 1913). Reprinted in New York *Call* (11 June 1913).

_____. "To the New College Girl." *The Youth's Companion* 79, no. 23 (8 June 1905): 275.

_____. "To the New York *Call.*" New York *Call* (7 September 1916).

_____. "To the Strikers at Little Falls, New York." *Solidarity* (21 November 1912).

_____. "The Training of a Blind Child." *Ladies Home Journal* (April 1908).

_____. "The True Religion." *Home Magazine* 6, no. 4 (1932): 6.

_____. "The Truth Again." *Ladies Home Journal* (January 1909).

_____. "Try Democracy." *Home Magazine* 11, no. 4 (1935): 11.

_____. "The Unbending Will." *Home Magazine* 6, no. 1 (1932): 6, 94.

_____. "The Unemployed Blind." *Ziegler Magazine for the Blind* (April 1911).

_____. "Unnecessary Blindness." *Ladies Home Journal* 24, no. 2 (1907): 14.

_____. "The Unprivileged." *Home Magazine* 4, no. 5 (1931): 8.

_____. "The Value of the Sense of Smell to the Blind-Deaf." *Outlook for the Blind* 4 (1910): 66–67.

_____. "A Vision of Service." *The New Church Messenger* 134, no. 25 (1928): 445–46.

_____. "Vision of Service." *Home Magazine* 7, no. 5 (1933): 6.

_____. "A Visit to Luther Burbank." *Outlook for the Blind* 19, no. 3 (1925): 21–24. Also in *Young People's Paper* 83, no. 6 (1926): 92.

_____. "The Voice of Humanity." *Home Magazine* 3, no. 6 (1931): 8, 109.

_____. *We Bereaved*. New York: Leslie Fulenwider, Inc., 1929.

_____. "We Can Do No More." *Home Magazine* 9, no. 2 (1934): 12.

_____. "We Don't Know How to Think." *Home Magazine* 1, no. 3 (1930): 7.

_____. "We Who Sit Apart." *Real Courage* 1, no. 3 (1924). Also in *Outlook for the Blind* 17, no. 4 (1924).

_____. "What Are Women Interested In?" *Home Magazine* 4, no. 3 (1931): 8.

_____. "What the Blind Can Do." *The Youth's Companion* 80, no. 1 (4 January 1906): 3–4.

_____. "What Is the IWW?" New York *Call* (3 February 1918).

_____. "What Might Be Done for the Blind." *World's Work* 14 (August 1907): 9259–64.

_____. "Why Men Need Woman Suffrage." New York *Call* (17 October 1915).

_____. "Why President Wilson Must Fail." New York *Call* (16 April 1913).

_____. "Wings." *Home Magazine* 12, no. 1 (1935): 16.

_____. "Women and Peace." *Home Magazine* 1, no. 2 (1930): 6.

_____. *The World I Live In*. New York: The Century Co., 1920.

_____. "The World Through Three Senses." *Ladies Home Journal*. In *Helen Keller: Newspaper Clippings and Pamphlets*. Washington, D.C.: Volta Bureau, n.d.

Keller, Helen Adams, and Harriet Stanton Blatch. "To President Woodrow Wilson: The Blockade of Russia." New York *Call* (21 December 1920).

Books and Articles About Helen Keller

The list below contains selected books and articles about Helen Keller:

Adler, David A. *A Picture Book of Helen Keller*. New York: Holiday House, 1990.

Alcorn, Sophia. "The Tadoma Method." *The Volta Review* (May 1932).

"The American Girl Who Won the Greatest Victory in All History." *New York American* (21 October 1904).

"American Mercury Salutes Helen Keller." *American Mercury* (September 1960).

America's Twelve Great Women Leaders During the Past Hundred Years as Chosen By the Women of America: A Compilation from the *Ladies Home Journal* and the *Christian Science Monitor*. Chicago: Associated Authors Service, 1933.

Anagnos, Michael. *Helen Keller*. Reprinted from the Report of the Perkins Institution, Boston: 1892.

_____, and Anne M. Sullivan. "Helen Keller's Early Life and First Instruction." *American Annals of the Deaf* (April 1988).

Anagnostopoulos, Michael. *Annual Reports of the Perkins Institution* (1887–1892).
_____. *Helen Keller, a Second Laura Bridgman*. Boston: Rand Avery, 1983.
"At 50, Helen Keller Is Hailed as a Marvel of Attainment." *Star* (22 June 1930).
Atkinson, Brooks. "'Miracle Worker': Two Strong Minds and Two Strong Players." Review of *The Miracle Worker*. *New York Times* (1 November 1959), sec. II: 1.
_____. "Theater: Giver of Light." Review of *The Miracle Worker*. *New York Times* (18 October 1959), sec. II: 1.
Avery, Constance D. "A Psychologist Looks at the Issue of Public vs. Residential School Placement for the Blind." *New Outlook for the Blind* 62 (September 1968): 221–26.
Barnett, M. Robert. "Helen Keller's Work for the American Foundation for the Blind." *New Outlook for the Blind* 62 (September 1968): 206–8.
Barrick, Mac E. "The Helen Keller Joke Cycle." *Journal of American Folklore* 93 (1980): 441–49.
Bartlett, Robert Merrill. *They Dared to Live*. New York: Association Press, 1943.
Beckley, Zoe. "Hearing Through Your Bones." *Helen Keller: Newspaper Clippings and Pamphlets*. Washington, D.C.: Volta Bureau, n.d.
Bell, Alexander Graham. Letter to Arthur Gilman (31 December 1897). Washington, D.C.: Volta Bureau.
_____. "The Method of Instruction Pursued with Helen Keller." *The Silent Educator* (June 1892).
Benjamin, Anne. *Young Helen Keller: Woman of Courage*. Mahwah, NJ: Troll Associates, 1992. "Recording."
Berkeley, George. *The Teaching of George Berkeley, Bishop of Cloyne*. Edited by A. A. Luce and T. E. Jessop. 9 vols. London: 1948.
Bigland, Eileen. *Helen Keller*. Springfield, MA: Phillips, 1967.
_____. *The True Book About Helen Keller*. London: F. Muller, 1957.
Bindley, Barbara. "Why I Became an IWW: An Interview with Helen Keller." New York *Tribune* (16 January 1916). Reprinted in "Helen Keller, Industrialist. Famous Blind Girl Says She Finds Party Too Slow and Is Now IWW Adherent." New York *Call* (17 January 1916).
"Bishop Brooks to Helen Keller." Boston *Transcript* (6 January 1892).
Blatt, Burton. "Friendly Letters on the Correspondence of Helen Keller, Anne Sullivan, and Alexander Graham Bell." *Exceptional Children* 51 (1985): 405–9.
Blaxall, Arthur William. *Helen Keller Under the Southern Cross*. Part I. Cape Town, South Africa: Juta and Company, Ltd., 1952.
"Blind and Deaf Girl: Story of Helen Keller's Wonderful Achievements." Washington *Evening Star* (3 January 1906).
Block, M., Ed. "Helen Keller." *Current Biography – 1942*. New York: The H.W. Wilson Co., 1942.
Bly, Nellie. "Deaf, Dumb, and Blind." *New York World* (17 February 1889).
Bolton, Sarah Knowles. *Lives of Girls Who Become Famous*. New York: Thomas Y. Crowell Company, 1914.
Booth, Miss Alice. "12 Greatest Living American Women." *Good Housekeeping* (1931).
Braddy, Nella. *Anne Sullivan Macy: The Story Behind Helen Keller*. New York: Doubleday, 1933.

Brake, Robert J., and Robert D. Neuleib. "Famous Women Orators: An Opinion Survey." *Today's Speech* 21, no. 4 (1973): 33–37.

Brooks, Van Wyck. "For the Blind." *New Outlook for the Blind* 62 (September 1968): 209–13.

_____. *Helen Keller: Sketch for a Portrait.* New York: E. P. Dutton and Co., Inc., 1956.

Brown, Marion, and Ruth Crone. *The Silent Story.* Nashville, TN: Abingdon: 1963.

Browne, Susan E., Debra Connors, and Nanci Stern, eds. *With the Power of Each Breath: A Disabled Women's Anthology.* Pittsburgh, PA: Cleis Press, 1985.

Bruce, Robert V. *Alexander Graham Bell: Teacher of the Deaf.* Northampton, MA: Clarke School for the Deaf, 1974.

_____. "A Conquest of Solitude." *American Heritage* 24, no. 3 (1973): 28–31, 96.

Brustein, Robert. "Two for the Miracle: Review of *The Miracle Worker.*" *New Republic* (9 November 1959): 28–29.

Bryan, Dorothy. "Work Opportunities for the Deaf-Blind." *Outlook for the Blind* (October 1949).

Cabot, Richard C. "Thank God for Helen Keller." *Survey* (1 April 1930).

Canby, Margaret T. *Birdie and His Fairy Friends: A Book for Little Children.* Philadelphia: Claxton, Remson and Haffelfinger, 1874.

Career Education. Washington, D.C.: U.S. Department of Health, Education, and Welfare, Office of Education, 1972.

Carnahan, Ann. "In an Exclusive Interview: Helen Keller at Age 80." *This Week* Magazine (19 June 1960).

Carratello, John. *Great Americans.* Huntington Beach, CA: Teacher Created Materials, 1991.

Cassirer, Ernst. *Essay on Man: An Introduction to a Philosophy of Human Culture.* New Haven, CT: Yale University Press, 1944.

Chambliss, Amy. "The Friendship of Helen Keller and Mark Twain." *Georgia Review* 24 (1970): 305–10.

Chappell, Jennie. *Always Happy: Or, The Story of Helen Keller.* London: S. W. Partridge and Co., 1890.

Coates, Florence Earle. "Helen Keller with a Rose." *Century Magazine* (July 1905): 397.

Coates, Robert M. "Helen Keller Profile." *New Yorker* (25 January 1930).

Cochrane, Orin. "How to Be a 'Miracle Worker.'" *Language Arts* 56 (May 1979): 534–38.

"College Course for Helen Keller." New York *Herald* (12 July 1895).

Collins, Louise Houk. *Helen Adams Keller: Her Life and Work.* M.A. thesis, n.p., 1940.

Combe, George. *Notes on the United States of North America During a Phrenological Visit in 1839–1840.* Philadelphia, PA: 1841.

A Conference of Hope: Proceedings of the Historic Helen Keller World Conference on Services to Deaf-Blind Youths and Adults. Louisville, KY: Department of Educational Research, 1977.

Coolidge, Susan. "Helen Keller." In *Last Verses.* Boston: Little, Brown and Company, 1906.

Copleston, Frederick, *A History of Philosophy.* Vol. 5 (Hobbes to Hume). Westminster, MD: The Newman Press, 1959.

Cotton, Carol. "Helen Keller's First Public Speech." *Alabama Historical Quarterly* 37 (1975): 68–72.

Critchell, Laurence. "The Day Helen Keller Came to Tokyo." *Saturday Evening Post* (25 February 1956): 31, 98.

Cunningham, Michael Gerald. "Remembering Helen Keller." New York: Seesaw Music, 1986. "Musical score."

Cutsforth, Thomas D. *The Blind in School and Society: A Psychological Study.* New York: D. Appleton and Company, 1933.

Dale, Bill. "Issues in Tramautic Blindness." *Journal of Visual Impairment and Blindness* 86 (1992): 140–43.

Daley, Jane B. "The Value of Vibration in Teaching Speech to the Deaf." *The Volta Review* (May 1932).

Davidson, Donald. *The Tennessee.* New York: Rinehart and Co., Inc., 1946.

Davidson, Margaret. *Helen Keller.* New York: Hastings House, 1971.

Davidson, Mickie. *Helen Keller's Teacher.* New York: Scholastic Book Services, 1965.

Davis, Fannie Stearns. "Of Helen Keller." *Good Housekeeping* (June 1910): 746.

De Felice, Robert J. "The Crippled Body Speaks." Ph.D. dissertation, State University of New York at Buffalo, 1990.

De Land, Fred. *Dumb No Longer: Romance of the Telephone.* Washington, D.C.: Volta Bureau, 1908, pp. 181–88.

_____. "Ever-Continuing Memorial." *The Educator* (September 1893): 117.

"Deliverance." *Outlook for the Blind* (17 September 1919): 83.

Dickens, Charles. *American Notes.* New York: Dutton, 1926.

Dinsmore, Annette B. *Methods of Communication with Deaf-Blind People.* New York: American Foundation for the Blind, Educational Series No. 5, 1953.

_____. "National Approach to the Education of Deaf-Blind Children." *New Outlook for the Blind* (January 1954).

"A Distinguished Lady—Portrait of Helen Keller." *Newsweek* (26 March 1956).

Dolin, Arnold. *Great American Heroines.* New York: Hart Publishing Company, 1960.

Drexler, Carol Joan. *Young Helen Keller.* Mahwah, NJ: Educational Reading Service, 1970.

Douglas, Emily Taft. *Remember the Ladies: The Story of Great Women Who Helped Shape America.* New York: G. P. Putnam's Sons, 1966, pp. 237–88.

Duffus, P.L. "At Eighty, the Miracle of Helen Keller." *New York Times Magazine* (26 June 1960).

Dunnahoo, Terry. *Annie Sullivan: A Portrait.* Chicago: Reilly and Lee Books, 1970.

Dyer, Donita. *Bright Promise: The Phenomenal Story of the Korean "Helen Keller."* Grand Rapids, MI: Zondervan Publishing House, 1983.

Ellis, William T. "Helen Keller and Tommy Stringer." *St. Nicholas* (October 1897): 996–1000.

Ethical Issues in the Field of Blindness: Papers Presented at the 1985 Helen Keller Seminar, 23–24 Oct. New York: American Foundation for the Blind, 1986.

"Evelyn Seide Walter, 88, Helen Keller Aide Obituary." New York *Times* (18 June 1988), sec. A: 32.

"Eyes and Ears in Her Fingers." New York *Herald* (10 November 1895).

Farrell, Gabriel. *Children of the Silent Night.* Watertown, MA: Perkins School for the Blind, 1956.

Fay, Edward Allen, ed. "How Helen Keller Acquired Language." *American Annals of the Deaf* (April 1892): 138–39.

Fenner, M. S. "Editor's Notebook." *NEA Journal* (November 1963).

Fillippeli, Susan E. "The Revolutionary Rhetoric of Helen Keller." M.A. thesis, University of Georgia, 1985.

Fish, Anna Gardner. *Perkins Institution and Its Deaf-Blind Pupils.* Watertown, MA: Perkins Institution and Massachusetts School for the Blind, 1934.

Foner, Philip, ed. *Helen Keller: Her Socialist Years.* New York: International Publishers, 1967.

French, Richard Slayton. *From Homer to Helen Keller.* New York: The American Foundation for the Blind, Inc., 1932.

Freudberg, David. "An Optimist In Spite of It All: Helen Keller's Life Story." Cambridge, MA: Sound Documentaries, 1993. Audio cassette.

Fuller, Sarah. "How Helen Keller Learned to Speak." *American Annals of the Deaf* (January 1892).

_____. *How Helen Keller Was Taught Speech.* Washington, D. C.: Volta Bureau, 1905.

"Gallant Lady Meets Herself When Young." *Life* (30 March 1962).

Garlick, Phyllis. *Conqueror of Darkness: The Story of Helen Keller.* London: Lutterworth Press, 1958.

Giantvalley, Scott. "A Spirit Not 'Blind to His Vision, Deaf to His Message': Helen Keller on Walt Whitman." *Walt Whitman Review* 28 (1982): 63–66.

Gibson, William. *The Miracle Worker: A Play for Television.* New York: Alfred A. Knopf, 1969.

_____. *Monday After the Miracle: A Play in Three Acts.* New York: Atheneum, 1983.

Giffin, Frederick C. "The Radical Vision of Helen Keller." *International Social Science Review* 59, no. 4 (1984): 27–32.

Gilder, Josephine B. "Miss Helen Keller as a Speaker." *Putnam's Monthly* (April 1907): 69–70.

Gilder, Richard Watson. "Of One Who Neither Sees Nor Hears (Helen Keller)." In *Poems of Richard Watson Gilder.* Boston: Houghton, 1908, pp. 278–79.

_____. "Two Optimists." *Century Magazine* (January 1905).

Gilman, Arthur. "Helen Keller at Cambridge." *Century Magazine* (January 1897): 473–75.

_____. Letter to William Wade (25 February 1898). Watertown, MA: Perkins Archives.

_____. *Miss Helen Keller's First Year of College Preparatory Work.* Washington, D. C.: Gibson Brothers, Printers, 1897.

Giovannitti, Arturo. "To Helen Keller." In *The Collected Poems of Arturo Giovannitti.* Chicago: 1962, p. 63.

"Good Companion—Helen Keller." *Life* (4 April 1960).

Good, Lin. Book review of *Helen and Teacher* by Joseph Lash. *Queen's Quarterly* 89 (spring 1982): 180–82.

Goodenough, Florence L. "Expression of the Emotions in a Blind-Deaf Child." *Journal of Abnormal and Social Psychology* (October-December 1932).

Gordon, Ruth. "The Day Helen Keller Came Backstage." In The New York Times *Great Lives of the Twentieth Century*. Edited by Arthur Gelb, A. M. Rosenthal, and Marvin Siegel, pp. 324–27. New York: Times Books, 1987.

Graff, Stewart. *Helen Keller: Toward the Light*. New Canaan, CT: Garrard, 1965.

Graff, Stewart, and Polly Anne Graff. *Helen Keller: Crusader for the Blind and Deaf*. New York: Dell Publishing, 1965.

Great American Women. Skokie, IL: Devco Publishers, 1981.

Great Personalities: Two as Reported in the New York Times. Sanford, NC: Microfilming Corporation of America, 1981.

"Great Photo Tells a Moving Story—Helen Keller's Fingers See the President's Smile." *Life* (16 November 1953).

Green, Katharine R. *Famous Women of the Western World*. Shanghai, China: Commercial Press, 1934.

Greene, Bob. "Her Life Was Not a Joke." *Chicago Tribune* (11 May 1992), sec. 5: 1.

Hagedorn, Hermann. *Americans: A Book of Lives*. New York: The John Day Company, 1946, pp. 267–90.

Hale, Edward Everett. "Helen Keller." *Outlook* (6 December 1902): 830–31.

———. "Helen Keller's Life." *Outlook* (22 June 1907): 379–83.

Hall, Florence. "Helen Keller." *St. Nicholas Magazine* (September 1889): 834–43.

———, and Marion Howe. *Helen Keller*. New York: 1889.

Hall, Inis B. "The Education of the Blind-Deaf." *The Volta Bureau* (October 1940).

Hannaford, Susan. *Living Outside Inside: A Disabled Woman's Experience*. Berkeley: Canterbury Press, 1985.

"Happy Children Once Mute, Now Bright Talkers." *Commercial Adviser*. New York (30 March 1895).

Harrity, Richard, and Ralph G. Martin. *The Three Lives of Helen Keller*. Garden City, NY: Doubleday and Company, Inc., 1962.

Harry, Gerald. *Man's Miracle: The Story of Helen Keller and Her European Sisters*. London: Heinemann, 1914.

Hayes, Richard. "Images: Review of *The Miracle Worker*." *Commonweal* (4 December 1959): 289.

Hedin, Laura. *Voices of Light and Grace: Reflections on the Lifework of Helen Keller and Anne Sullivan Macy*.

Heidt, Edward R. "Narrative Voice in Autobiographical Writing." Ph.D. dissertation, University of Southern California, 1989.

"Helen Adams Keller: An Appreciation." *Pictorial Review* (January 1933).

"Helen Keller." *The Educator* 4 (October 1893).

"Helen Keller." [s.l.] Official Films, 1963. Film reel.

"Helen Keller." Princeton, NJ: Films for the Humanities, 1988. Videocassette.

"Helen Keller." Chicago: Questar Video, 1991. Videocassette.

"Helen Keller." Northbrook, IL: Coronet Film and Video, 1990. Videocassette and Discussion Guide.

"Helen Keller." *Current Biography* (1942).

"Helen Keller." *Lend a Hand* (March 1888): 137–46.

"Helen Keller—1880–1968." *The New Outlook for the Blind* 62 (September 1968): 202–5.

Helen Keller: America's Disabled. Piterborough, NH: Piterborough Magazine, 1983.

"Helen Keller Aide for 37 Years." *Chicago Tribune* (18 June 1988).

"Helen Keller and Her Pupil." New York *Sun* (4 June 1913).

"Helen Keller and Her Teacher." Videocassette. [S.I.] McGraw-Hill Films, 1970.

"Helen Keller and the Dog." Boston *Herald* 32 (1 February 1902).

"Helen Keller, Deaf-Blind Marvel. In *When They Were Young Series.* Columbus, OH: School and College Service, 1969.

"Helen Keller Dies." *New York Times* (2 June 1968).

"Helen Keller Heartbroken at Failure to Get Degree." *Boston Post* (25 June 1904).

"Helen Keller in Cambridge." *The Critic* (14 November 1896): 303.

"Helen Keller in Her Story." New York: American Foundation for the Blind Videos, 1900. Videocassette.

"Helen Keller Interview." In New Bedford *Sunday Standard* (22 November 1914).

"Helen Keller Points to Social Enemies." New York *Call* (15 February 1911).

"Helen Keller—Portrait." *Newsweek* (18 November 1953).

"Helen Keller—Portrait." *Newsweek* (8 July 1957).

"Helen Keller—Portrait." *Time* (16 November 1953).

"Helen Keller: Separate Views." New York: Master Vision, 1982. Videocassette.

"Helen Keller: The World I See." Arts and Entertainment "Biography" (28 November 1989). Television Program.

"Helen Keller to Defy Jingoes." New York *Call* (2 January 1916).

"Helen Keller—Unconquered." *Time* (12 July 1954).

The Helen Keller World Conference on Services to Deaf-Blind Persons. Stockholm, Sweden, 28 September – 3 October 1989.

"Helen Keller's Feat." *Truth* (16 July 1896).

"Helen Keller's Story of My Life." *Atlantic Monthly* (June 1903): 842–43.

Henderson, Lois T. *The Opening Doors: My Child's First Eight Years Without Sight.* New York: The John Day Company, 1954.

Henny, Nella Braddy. *Anne Sullivan Macy: The Story Behind Helen Keller.* New York: Doubleday, 1933.

_____. "Helen Keller." *New York Times Magazine* (26 June 1955).

_____. *With Helen Keller.* North Conway, NH: North Conway Publishing Co., 1974.

Hewes, Henry. "The Miracle at Work: Review of *The Miracle Worker.*" *Saturday Review* (7 November 1959): 28.

Hickok, Lorena A. *The Story of Helen Keller.* New York: Grosset and Dunlap, 1958.

_____. *The Touch of Magic: The Story of Helen Keller's Great Teacher, Anne Sullivan Macy.* New York: Dodd, Mead and Company, 1961.

"A Hit at 10: Review of *The Miracle Worker.*" *Newsweek* (2 November 1959): 97.

Hitz, John. "Helen Keller." *American Anthropologist* 8, no. 2 (April–June 1906): 308–24.

_____. Letter to Alexander Graham Bell (27 December 1897). Washington, D. C.: Volta Bureau.

Hogrogian, Robert. "Helen Keller." Hawthorne, NJ: January Productions, 1981. Recording.

Horner, Matina S. "Remember the Ladies." In *Helen Keller* by Dennis Wepman. New York: Chelsea House Publishers, 1987, pp. 7–10.

Houston, Jean. *Public Like a Frog: Entering the Lives of Three Great Americans.* Wheaton, IL: Quest Books, 1993.

Howe, Julia Ward. *Reminiscences 1819–1899.* Boston: Houghton, 1899.

Howe, Maud, and Florence Howe Hall. *Laura Bridgman: Dr. Howe's Famous Pupil and What He Taught Her.* Boston: Little, Brown and Company, 1904.

Hughes, Carol. "Helen Keller: The Unconquerable." *Coronet* 22, no. 1 (May 1947): 130–38.

Hull, John M. *Touching the Rock: An Experience of Blindness.* Pantheon, 1991.

Hunter, Nigel. *Helen Keller.* New York: The Bookwright Press, 1986.

Huntoon, B. B. Letter to Arthur Gilman (14 February 1898). Watertown, MA: Perkins Archives.

Hutton, Eleanor. Letter to Arthur Gilman (9 December 1897). Watertown, MA: Perkins Archives.

Hytten, Ella. *Helen Keller.* Oslo: E. G. Mortensen, 1961.

"In a Silent World." *Current Literature* (April 1903): 406.

"In Regard to Helen Keller." *The Critic* (17 April 1897): 277.

Jaendicks, Martin. *Helen Keller.* Berlin: Union-Verlag, 1972.

Jastrow, Joseph. "Psychological Notes on Helen Kellar [*sic*]." *Psychological Review* 1 (1894): 356–62.

_____. "The Story of Helen Keller." *The Dial* (16 April 1903): 1–5.

Johnson, Ann Donegan. *The Value of Determination: The Story of Helen Keller.* La Jolla, CA: Value Communications, Inc., 1976.

Johnson, Patty. *Helen Keller: Girl from Alabama.* Huntsville, AL: Strode Publishers, 1980.

Jolly, William. *Education: Its Principles and Practice as Developed by George Combe.* London: Macmillan and Company, 1879.

Jones, Susan, ed. "Helen Keller, Voice and Vision in the Soul." Van Nuys, CA: AIMS Media, 1986. Interactive Video and Discussion Guide.

Keith, Merton S. "Final Preparation for College." *Helen Keller Souvenir No. 2 1892–1899.* Washington, D. C.: Volta Bureau, 1899, pp. 34–59.

Kelton, Nancy. *The Finger Game Miracle.* Milwaukee, WI: Raintree Publishers, 1977.

Kennedy, Patricia Scileppi, and Gloria Hartmann O'Shields. *We Shall Be Heard: Women Speakers in America, 1828-Present.* Dubuque, IA: Kendall/Hunt Publishing Company, 1983, pp. 245–57.

Kessler, Rikki. *Helen Keller by Stewart and Polly Anne Graff: Study Guide.* Roslyn Heights, NY: Learning Links, 1982.

Kinscella, Hazel Gertrude. "Helen Keller Sees Flowers and Hears Music." In *Helen Keller: Newspaper Clippings and Pamphlets.* Washington, D. C.: Volta Bureau, n.d.: 33 and 112.

Klages, Mary Krag. "More Wonderful Than Any Fiction: The Representation of Helen Keller." Ph.D. dissertation, Stanford University, 1989.

Koestler, Frances A. *The Unseen Minority: A Social History of Blindness in America.* New York: David McKay Company, Inc., 1976.

Kudlinski, Kathleen V. *Helen Keller: A Light for the Blind.* New York: Puffin Books, 1991.

Lamson, Mary Swift. *Life and Education of Laura Dewey Bridgman: The Deaf, Dumb, and Blind Girl.* Boston: Houghton, Mifflin, and Company, 1892.

Lash, Joseph P. *Helen and Teacher: The Story of Helen Keller and Anne Sullivan Macy.* New York: Delacorte Press, 1980.

_____. *Helen and Teacher: The Story of Helen Keller and Anne Sullivan Macy—Annotated Edition.* New York: Delacorte Press, 1980. Washington, D. C.: Volta Bureau, 1980. Also available at the American Foundation for the Blind, the Perkins Institution, and the Schlesinger Library of Ratliffe College.

_____. "Helen Keller: Movie Star." *American Heritage* 31, no. 3 (1980): 76–85.

_____. "Keller, Helen." In *Notable American Women.* Edited by Barbara Sicherman and Carol Hurd Green. Vol. 4: 389–93. Cambridge, MA: Belknap Press of Harvard University Press, 1980.

"Laura Bridgman." *The Christian Observatory* (March 1847): 130–39.

LeBlanc, Georgette. *The Girl Who Found the Blue Bird: A Visit to Helen Keller.* Translated by Alexander Teixeira De Mattos. New York: Dodd, Mead and Company, 1914.

"A Life of Joy." *Time* (7 June 1968): 30.

Locher, F., ed. "Helen Keller." In *Contemporary Authors.* Vol. 101. Detroit, MI: Gale Research Co., 1981.

Lotz, Philip Henry. *Women Leaders.* New York: Association Press, 1940.

Lowenfeld, Berthold. "Helen Keller: A Remembrance." *Journal of Visual Impairment and Blindness* 74 (May 1980): 169–74.

_____. "If Deaf and Blind." *California Parent-Teacher* (April 1952).

MacDonald, A. B. "Visiting the Kansas Deaf and Blind Girl to Whom Miss Helen Keller Has Paid High Tribute." The Kansas City *Times* (9 April 1933).

Mackenzie, Catherine. *Alexander Graham Bell: The Man Who Contracted Space.* New York: Grosset and Dunlap, Inc., 1928.

Macy, John Albert. "Helen Keller as She Really Is." *Ladies Home Journal* (October–November, 1902): 11, 12, 40.

_____. "Helen Keller's Critics." Boston *Evening Transcript* (27 May 1903), part II: 22.

_____. *The Spirit of American Literature.* New York: Doubleday, 1913.

Maifair, Linda Lee. *People and Places.* Laguna Niguel, CA: Monkey Sisters, 1989.

Mannix, John Bernard. *Heroes of the Darkness.* London: S. W. Partridge and Company, Ltd., 1911.

"Mark Twain, George Bernard Shaw, Helen Keller." Norwalk, CT: Easton Press Video, 1988. Videocassette.

Markham, Lois. *Helen Keller.* New York: F. Watts, 1993.

Martin, Paul. "Helen Keller's Knights of the Blind." In *We Serve: A History of the Lions Clubs.* Washington, D. C.: Regnery Gateway, 1991, pp. 55–62.

"Marvelous Is Helen Keller." New York *Herald* (19 December 1894).

Matthews, Gwyneth Ferguson. *Voices from the Shadows: Women with Disabilities Speak Out.* Toronto: Women's Education Press, 1983.

Melder, Keith. *Beginnings of Sisterhood: The American Women's Rights Movement, 1800–1850.* New York: Schocken Books, 1977.

Merry, Ralph V. "A Case Study in Deaf-Blindness." *Journal of Abnormal and Social Psychology* (July–September 1930).

"The Miracle Worker." Culver City, CA: MGM/UA Home Video, 1992. Videocassette.

"Miracles of Today." *Lend a Hand* (May 1893): 357–68.

"Miss Helen Keller on How Women Should Dress." Boston *Morning Post* (23 February 1913).

"Miss Keller's Autobiography." *The Independent* (30 April 1903): 1033–34.

"Miss Sullivan's Methods." anon. ts. Watertown, MA: Perkins Archives.

Montague, Harriet Andrews. "Penetrating the Darkness." In *Helen Keller: Newspaper Clippings and Pamphlets.* Washington, D. C.: Volta Bureau, November 1930.

Montgomery, L. M. *Courageous Women.* New York: Trumpet Club, 1991.

Moore, Rebecca Deming. *When They Were Girls.* Dansville, NY: F. A. Owen Publishing Company, 1937.

Morris, Harvey. "The Unhelped Blind." *New Outlook for the Blind* 62 (September 1968): 227–29.

Moulton, Robert H. "School Days with Helen Keller." *Survey Graphic* (May 1936).

Murray, Don. "What Do You Mean by 'Hopeless'?" *The Saturday Evening Post* (2 March 1957).

Myklebust, Helmer R. *The Deaf-Blind Child.* Watertown, MA: Perkins School for the Blind, 1956.

"Negro Leaders Hail Helen Keller." *Negro History Bulletin* (March 1955).

Neilson, William Allan. Review of "Helen Keller's *Story of My Life.*" *Atlantic Monthly*, 91 (June 1903): 842–44.

Nelson, Nancy J. "A Critical Analysis of Helen Keller's Socialist Speaking." Unpublished M.A. Thesis, South Dakota University, 1984.

"New Plays on Broadway: Review of *The Miracle Worker.*" *Time* (2 November 1959): 30.

Newspaper Clippings and Pamphlets. Washington, D.C.: Volta Bureau, n.d.

Newton, A. E. "Westward." *Atlantic Monthly* (May 1932).

Peare, Catherine Owens. *The Helen Keller Story.* New York: Thomas Y. Crowell Company, 1959.

Percy, Walker. "The Delta Factor." *The Message in the Bottle.* New York: Farrar, 1954.

Perry, Adeline G. "A Visit from Helen Keller." *St. Nicholas* (June 1892): 573–77.

Peterson, Houston. *Great Teachers Portrayed by Those Who Studied Under Them.* New Brunswick, NJ: Rutgers University Press, 1946.

Pitkin, Walter B. "Who Among Living Americans Ranks Highest in Achievement?" *Helen Keller: Newspaper Clippings and Pamphlets.* Washington, D.C.: Volta Bureau, n.d.

Polcover, Jane. *Helen Keller.* Chicago: Children's Press Choice, 1988.

Pollard, Michael. *People Who Care.* Ada, OK: Garrett Educational Corp., 1992.

Porter, Edna, Comp. *Double Blossoms: Helen Keller Anthology.* New York: Lewis Copeland, 1931.

"The Religion of Helen Keller." *Current Literature* (December 1908): 645–48.

Richards, Laura. *Samuel Gridley Howe.* New York: D. Appleton-Century Co., 1935.

Richards, Norman. *People of Destiny: Helen Keller.* Chicago: Children's Press, 1968.

Robertson, Nan. "Broadway Slugging Match: Review of *The Miracle Worker.*" *New York Times* (20 December 1959), sec. II: 5.

Rocheleua, Corinne and Rebecca Mack. *Those in the Dark Silence*. Washington, D.C.: The Volta Bureau, 1930.

Rogow Lee. "Miss Keller for Posterity." *Saturday Review* (12 June 1954): 26.

Ross, Ishbel. "The Extraordinary Helen Keller: Portrait at 70." *Subject and Strategy: A Rhetoric Reader*. Eds. Paul Eschholz and Alfred Rosa. 5th ed. New York: St. Martin's Press, 1990, pp. 97–108.

_____. "The Extraordinary Story of Helen Keller." *Reader's Digest* (July 1950): 161–68.

_____. *Journey into Light: The Story of the Education of the Blind*. New York: Appleton-Century-Crofts, Inc., 1951.

Royce, Josiah. *The Spirit of Modern Philosophy*. Boston: Houghton, Mifflin and Company, 1897.

Sabin, Francene. *The Courage of Helen Keller*. Mahwah, NJ: Troll Associates, 1982.

_____. "The Courage of Helen Keller." Sound Cassette. Mawhah, NJ: Troll Associates, 1983.

Salerno, Joan. "Heroes in Books." *Media and Methods* 17 (September 1980): 35–37.

Salmon, Peter J. *The Worcester Lad Fondly Remembers Helen Keller on the Centennial Celebration of Her Birth, June 27, 1980*. New York: Industrial Home for the Blind, 1980.

Santrey, Laurence. *Helen Keller*. Sound Cassette. Mahwah, NJ: Troll Associates, 1985.

Saul, E. Wendy. "Living Proof: What Helen Keller, Marilyn Monroe, and Marie Curie Have in Common." *School-Library-Journal* 33 (October 1986): 103–8.

Schlossberg, Hattie. "Helen Keller: An Appreciation." *New York Call* (4 May 1913): 15.

"School Opened Here to Teach Only Deaf-Blind." *New York Herald Tribune* (9 March 1938).

Schwartz, Harold. *Samuel Gridley Howe*. Cambridge: Harvard University Press, 1956.

Scouten, Edward L. *Turning Points in the Education of Deaf People*. Danville, IL: The Interstate Printers and Publishers, Inc., 1988, pp. 230–42.

"Sees with Her Soul." Washington *Evening News* (22 July 1893).

Shanks, Ann Zane. *Helen Keller: Voice and Vision in the Soul*. Chatzworth, CA: AIMS Media, 1986. Videocassette.

Sioui, Eleandre Marie Andatha. "A Huron-Wyandot Woman's Life Story: The Realization of an Impossible Dream." Unpublished Ph.D. dissertation, The Union for Experimenting Colleges and Universities, 1988.

Sloan, Carolyn. *Helen Keller*. London: Evans Brothers, Ltd., 1992.

Smith, B. "Walk with Helen Keller." *Cosmopolitan* (December 1954).

Smithdas, Robert. *Life at My Fingertips*. Garden City, NY: Doubleday and Company, Inc., 1958.

Socialization: Selected Readings for Unit II. Minneapolis, MN: Project Social Studies of the University of Minnesota, 1966.

Soler, Blanch C. *Helen Keller*. Barcelona, Spain: Ediciones AFHA Internacional, 1968.

St. George, Judith. *Dear Dr. Bell: Your Friend, Helen Keller*. New York: G. P. Putnam's Sons, 1992.

Staples, B. "When They Were Young." In *Helen Keller*. Columbus, OH: School Speciality Press, 1931.

State of the Blindness System Today: 1887–1890. Helen Keller Seminars. New York: American Foundation for the Blind, 1992. Recording.

Stedman, Edmund Clarence. "Helen Keller" (poem). *American Annals of the Deaf* (January 1891).

_____. "Helen Keller." In *Poems of Edmund Clarence Stedman*. Boston: Houghton, 1908, pp. 450–51.

Stoddard, Hope. *Famous American Women*. New York: Thomas Y. Crowell Company, 1970, pp. 234–44.

"Story of Helen Keller." *Life* (21 June 1954).

Sullivan, Anne M. "How Helen Keller Acquired Language." *American Annals of the Deaf*, 37, no. 2 (April 1892).

Sullivan, Anne M., M. Anagnos, and Job Williams. "Helen Keller's Story of the Frost King." *American Annals of the Deaf*, 37, no. 2 (April 1892).

Sutton, Estella V. "Helen Keller, the Blind and Deaf Phenomenon." *Education* (February 1894): 341–50.

Swanson, Virginia. *The Power of Overcoming: Featuring the Story of Helen Keller*. Provo, UT: Eagle Systems Intern, 1984. Recording.

_____. *The Story of Helen Keller*. Antioch, CA: Eagle Systems International, 1984.

Tames, Richard. *Helen Keller*. New York: Franklin Watts, 1991.

Taylor, Eugene. "William James and Helen Keller." An address delivered at the 156th General Convention of the Swedenborgian Churches, Wellesley College, 26 June 1980.

"Teaching the Deaf to Speak." *Scientific American*. New York City (9 January 1892).

Tedder, Norma. "They're Not All Helen Kellers." *Readings in Deafness* 8 (May 1983): 17–20.

Thomas, Henry, and Dana Lee Thomas. *50 Great Americans: Their Inspiring Lives and Achievements*. Garden City, NY: Doubleday and Company, Inc., 1948. pp. 414–20.

Thompson, Carol D. "Controversies in the Socialist Party: An Open Letter to Helen Keller." New York *Call* (22 February 1913): 9.

Tilney, Dr. Frederick. "The Mind of Helen Keller." *Personality* (October 1928).

"The Time Helen Keller Played the Palace [June 1962]." In *The New York Times Great Lives of the Twentieth Century*. Edited by Arthur Gelb, A. M. Rosenthal, and Marvin Siegel. New York: Times Books, 1987, pp. 327–28.

Trobridge, George. *Swedenborg: Life and Teaching*. New York: The Swedenborg Foundation, Inc., 1955.

Vance, W. Silas. "The Teacher of Helen Keller." *The Alabama Review* 24, no. 1 (1971): 51–62.

Villey, Pierre. *The World of the Blind*. New York: The Macmillan Company, 1930.

Wade, Mary Hazelton Blanchard. *The Wonder-Workers*. Boston: Little, 1916.

Wade, William. Letter to Arthur Gilman (29 November 1897). Watertown, MA: Perkins Archives.

_____. Letter to Arthur Gilman (14 December 1897). Watertown, MA: Perkins Archives.

_____. Letter to Arthur Gilman (4 January 1898). Watertown, MA: Perkins Archives.

Waite, Helen E. *Valiant Companions: Helen Keller and Anne Sullivan Macy*. Philadelphia, PA: Macrae Smith Co., 1959.

Walter, Erich, A. *1993 Essay Annual: A Yearly Collection of Significant Essays, Personal, Critical, Controversial, and Humorous*. Chicago: Scott, Foresman, 1993.

Wepman, Dennis. *Helen Keller: Humanitarian*. New York: Chelsea House Publishers, 1987.

"When Helen Keller Met Montessori." *Literary Digest*, 48: (17 January 1914): 134ff.

"Where Americans Are Made." Boston *Sunday Globe* (17 May 1903).

White, Sallie Joy. "The Story of Helen Keller." *Wide Awake* (July 1888): 77–85.

Whitman, Alden. "Helen Keller: Biographical Essay." In *The New York Times Great Lives of the Twentieth Century*. Edited by Arthur Gelb, A. M. Rosenthal, and Marvin Siegel. New York: Times Books, 1987, pp. 318–24.

_____. *Triumph Out of Tragedy*. New York: American Foundation for the Blind, 1980.

Whitman, Mrs. Bernard. "Helen Keller." *Lend a Hand* (April 1889): 289–303.

Whitten, Laurie Lee. "Actress Choices for Helen Keller in Monday After the Miracle." M.F.A. thesis, Texas Tech University, 1986.

Whitty, Pam. "A Reclamation of the Educational Thought of Helen Keller: Her Journey from 'No-World' to 'World Home.'" Ed.D. dissertation, University of Maine at Orono, 1993.

"Who Is Stanislavsky? Review of *The Miracle Worker*." *Time* (21 December 1959): 46–48+.

Whorf, Mike. *The Luminous World of Helen Keller*. Birmingham, MI: Mike Whorf, Inc., 1970. sound recording.

Wilkie, Katherine Elliott. *Helen Keller: From Tragedy to Triumph*. New York: The Bobbs-Merrill Co., Inc., 1969.

William, John, and Anne Tibble. *Helen Keller: Lives to Remember*. London: Adam and Charles Black, 1957.

Wilson, P. W. "The Liberator of Helen Keller." New York *Times* (1 October 1933).

Winerip, Michael. "Elysian Days at Helen Keller: A Special Day Camp." New York *Times* (31 July 1987), sec. B: 1.

"Woman Who Liberated the Mind of Helen Keller: Theme of a New Book." New York *Times* (10 October 1933).

Woollcott, Alexander. "In Memoriam: Annie Sullivan." *Atlantic Monthly* (March 1939).

Years of Triumph: Helen Keller. Friends of the Libraries: University of Southern California, 1970.

Yelverton, Mildred G. *They Also Served: Twenty-five Remarkable Alabama Women*. Dothan, AL: Ampersand Publishers, 1993.

Young, Iola S. "Helen Keller Came." *The Pacific Historian* 24, no. 1 (1980): 55–59.

Zahl, Paul A., ed. *Blindness: Modern Approaches to the Unseen Environment*. Princeton, NJ: Princeton University Press, 1950.

Keller at 80 years old. Age gave her wisdom. She possessed spark and enthusiasm both as a young girl and as an elderly woman.

Index

Absolute language, 61

Abstract terms, 13–14, 20, 62–63

Action steps, 30, 85–87, 88–90, 93–94, 96, 98, 99, 103, 119–120

"Address in St. Bride's Parish Church," 6, 36, 41, 115, 123

"Address of Helen Keller at Mt. Airy," 5, 14, 15, 16, 35, 80–81, 123

"Address to the National Council of Women," 6, 34, 37, 118, 123

"Address to the National Institute for the Blind," 6, 37, 42, 116–117, 123

"Address to the New Church of Scotland" (Swedenborgian), 6, 36, 114, 123

"Address to the Rotarians of Inverness," 34, 40, 123

"Address to the Teachers of the Deaf and of the Blind," 6, 36, 42, 111–112, 123

Alexander Graham Bell Association for the Deaf (also known as the Volta Bureau), 7

American Annals of the Deaf, 15

American Foundation for Overseas Blind, 119

American Foundation for the Blind, 6, 43, 68, 72, 109–110, 125, 131, 134, 138, 145

Anagnos, Michael, 24, 50, 58, 137, 138, 148

Analogies and associations, 38, 57, 61, 62–63

Archetypal metaphors, xviii, 31–39, 41

Archives of materials on Helen Keller, 6–7, 131

Arnold, Carroll C., 39, 127

Articulation, 14

Auden, W. H., 33, 127

Audiences of Keller's speeches, 41, 42–43

Behaviorism, 65–66

Bell, Alexander Graham, 14, 138, 139, 143, 145, 147

Berkeley, Bishop George, 65–66, 128, 138

Biblical references, xxi, 11, 15, 41–42, 75, 114, 115

The Blind in School and Society, 52

Blindness, used as metaphor, 21, 95, 107

Boston's *Home Journal*, 70

Braddy, Nella, 45, 127, 136, 138, 143

Braille, 2, 16, 75, 119

Braille-writer, xxii, 22, 72

Braun, John Elliott, 128

Bridgman, Laura, 14, 51, 66, 125, 127, 144, 145

Brooklyn *Eagle*, 56

Burden of proof, 56–57

Burke, Kenneth, xviii, 125

The Call, 131, 132, 134, 136, 137, 138

Cambridge School for Young Ladies, 20

Canby, Margaret T., 50, 139

Cassirer, Ernst, 65, 128, 139

Century Dictionary, 60

Century Magazine, 128, 131, 136

"A Chant of Darkness," 126, 131

Characteristics of speaking, 23–44, 126–127

Chautauqua lecture circuit, 22, 43

Cherokee teachings, 38

Childhood, influence of first 19 months, 66–67
Combe, George, 51, 52, 127, 144
"Commencement Address to Queen Margaret College," 6, 26, 36, 113, 123
Communication as inquiry, 65
Communism, 49
"The Conservation of Eyesight," 5, 29, 35, 91–92, 123
Conundrums used by Keller, 17
Creation stories, 37–38
Criticisms of Keller, 4, 45–53, 128, 145
Cutsforth, Thomas D., 52–53, 127, 140

Darwin, Charles, 54, 95
Deafness, used as metaphor, 21, 87, 95
Debate whether blind people should speak or use sign language, 15
Debs, Eugene V., 107, 136
Deliberative speaking, 73
Deliverance, 43
Delivery, 15, 43, 134
Delta factor, 12–13, 146
Descartes, Rene, 53, 56
Diderot, Denis, 60, 128
Disease and cure images, 33, 34

Education, 18–21, 37, 52–53, 58–59, 62, 127, 137, 138, 148
"The Education of the Blind," 123
Effects of Keller's speeches, 5, 7, 71–74, 75
Emerson, Ralph Waldo, 65
Epideictic speaking, 73
Eye banks, 72

Familial images, 33, 96
Figurative language, 45, 50
Fillippeli, Susan E., 31, 48–49, 68, 126, 127, 129
Finger spelling, 2, 12
Foner, Philip, 126, 127, 128, 129, 133, 141
Foreign Blind Association, 86
"The Frost Fairies," 50

The Frost King incident, 49–51, 58–59, 148
Fuller, Miss Sarah, 14, 80, 141
Fundraising campaigns, 71–72, 109–110, 119–120

"Genesis," 37
"The Gift of Language," 5, 18, 36, 40, 67, 93–94, 123
Glasgow, 111–112, 113, 114
Goodson Gazette, 51
Greek mythology, 42

Hand imagery, 27–28, 35, 60–61
"The Hand of the World," 27–28, 126, 132
Harding, President Warren, 17
"The Heart and the Hand," 76, 123
"The Heaviest Burden of the Blind," 5, 35, 88–90, 132
Helen and Teacher, 4, 6
Helen Keller Archives, 7, 125
Helen Keller Eye Research Foundation, 131
Helen Keller in Scotland, 127, 133
Henny, Nella Braddy. *See* Braddy, Nella
Holland, 72
Hollywood, 23
Horace, 25
Horace Mann School for the Deaf, 14
"How I Became a Socialist," 126, 133
Howe, Samuel Gridley, 6, 7–8, 18, 51, 52, 85, 146
Humanitarian, 23–24, 40–41, 43, 44
Humor, 6, 17

Idealism, 18, 65–66
Identification with listeners, 39
Imagery,
    Conflict between good and evil, 24–25, 43–44, 74, 118
    Freedom versus slavery, 16–17
    Light versus darkness, 25–26, 31, 43–44, 95–96, 104–105, 109, 114
    Social blindness and social deafness, 21, 26–27, 31
    Socialism versus capitalism, 28–31

Visual and auditory, 45, 51
Water and the sea, 32–33, 120
Imagination, 61, 62
Importance of education, 24
Index to Journals in Communication Studies Through 1995, 4
India, 72
Industrial Blindness and Social Deafness, 27
Industrial Workers of the World (IWW), 7, 30, 31, 43, 123, 126, 133, 137, 138
Intellectual images, 39
International Convention of Lions Clubs International, 6

James, William, 53, 65, 71, 148
Joan of Arc, 8
Jolly, William, 127, 144

Kant, Immanuel, 65–66, 129
Kautsky, Karl, 54
Keith, Merton S., 144
Keller, Helen,
   Birth, 3, 9
   Change from peaceful to revolutionary rhetoric, 23, 24–31
   Characteristics of her speaking, 4, 23–44
   Death, 75, 143
   Discovery of language, 3, 11–21, 75, 106, 141, 148
   Dreams, 66
   Early years, 3, 9–11, 66–67
   Effects of her speaking, 5, 7, 71–74, 75
   How rhetorical issues paralleled personal issues, 30, 31, 67–69
   Ideas about the supremacy of the soul, 63–66
   Idyllic world view, 18, 24
   Imagery, 16–17, 24–39
   Importance of education, 18–20
   Importance of imagination, 19
   Importance of language, 9, 21, 93
   Importance of speaking, 14, 18, 20, 67, 80–81, 93–94

   Justifying her right to speak, 31, 45, 53–66, 67–69, 82, 95, 99
   Lecturer, 18
   Mature woman, vi, 6, 121, 130, 150
   Revolutionary rhetoric, 5, 7–8, 24–31, 43–44, 45, 48
   Stressing similarities to sighted and hearing people, 53–55, 57–59
   Writer, 18
Kellog Foundation, 119
Kindergarden for the Blind, 87
Kipling, Rudyard, 90
Klages, Mary Krag, 51–52, 125, 127, 144
Knights of the Blind, 6, 71–72, 110, 119–120, 134, 145

La Follette, Robert M., 55–56, 129
Language, importance of, 9–21
Language, learning, 9, 10, 11, 12, 13, 14
Language as metaphor, 63
Lash, Joseph P., 4, 6, 24, 50, 52–53, 68, 125, 126, 127, 128, 129, 145
Lautsky, Karl, 54, 95
Learning by association, 38
Lectures, 43, 76, 134
Lions Clubs International, 6, 71–72, 109–110, 119–120, 125, 129, 131, 145
Lip-reading, xxii, 2, 14, 16,
Lodge, Sir Oliver, 54, 95
Love, Dr. James Kerr, 66–67, 129, 133

Macy, Anne Sullivan. *See* Sullivan, Anne
Macy, John, 59, 128, 145
Manual alphabet, xxii, 2, 12, 14, 16
Marx, Karl, 54, 95
Marxist rhetoric, 42
Massachusetts Association for Promoting the Interests of the Adult Blind, 5, 82, 135
Materialistic philosophy of language, 51–52

"Menace of the Militarist Program," 5, 28–29, 36, 40, 97–98, 123, 126, 134
Metaphors, 21
Midstream: My Later Life, 53, 127, 128, 129, 134
Military hospitals, 43, 73
The Miracle Worker, 5, 43, 68, 138, 139, 141, 142, 143, 146
Montessori, Maria, 149
My Key of Life, 126, 129, 134. *See also Optimism*
My Religion, 41, 64–65, 125, 128, 134
Mysticism, 42

National Council of Women, 118
National Institute for the Blind, 37, 116–117
Nature images, 34–35
Nelson, Nancy J., 125, 146
"A New Light Is Coming," 5, 25, 26, 27, 33, 36, 54, 95–96, 123, 126, 135
"New Vision for the Blind," 126, 135
New York *Nation,* 48
New York *Post,* 48

O'Hare, Kate, 107
"Onward, Comrades!" 5, 25, 33, 34–35, 36, 40, 104–105, 123, 135
Optimism, 32, 35–37
Optimism, 35, 135. *See also My Key of Life*
Osborn, Michael, M., 31–34, 126, 127
"Our Duties to the Blind," 5, 30, 34, 35, 53–54, 82–87, 123, 135
Out of the Dark, 127, 127, 128, 135

Pacifist rhetoric, 7, 23, 34, 43, 45
Peirce, C. S., 65
Percy, Walter, 12, 125, 146
Perkins School for the Blind, 5, 7, 12, 20, 24, 50, 58, 82, 83, 84, 85, 87, 89, 125, 126, 127, 128, 131, 135, 137, 138, 141, 145
Phantom, 11, 13, 20
The Philosophy of Rhetoric, 63, 128
Phrenologists, 51

Pilkilton, Sue, xxiv
"The Plain Truth," 123
Plato, 65
Playing with words, 17
Pragmatism, 65–66

Ratcliffe College, 20, 65, 75, 145
Religious language, 41–42, 61, 79, 114, 115, 117
Response to criticisms, 53–66
Rhetorical questions, 40, 56–57, 98, 100
Richards, I. A., 63, 128
Romantic poetry, 33, 42
Roosevelt, Eleanor, 23
Royce, Josiah, 65–66, 128, 147

Sarcasm, 55
Schlesinger Library at Ratcliffe College, 7, 131, 145
Sense of smell, 35, 47, 48, 59–60, 61–62, 75, 127, 137
Sense of taste, 48, 60, 61, 62, 75
Sense of touch, 27–28, 47, 48, 60–61, 62, 75
Sensory images, 39, 45, 50, 51–52
Shaw, George Bernard, 54, 95, 132, 145
SightFirst program, 72
Sign language, 15, 75
Socialist rhetoric, 4, 5, 7, 25–26, 26–31, 43, 45, 49, 56, 66, 67, 73, 74, 133
Socrates, 66
Speaking, learning to, 14, 15, 20
"Speech at Andover," 5, 35, 75, 123
"Speech to Annual Convention of Lions Clubs International," 36, 109–110, 123
"Speech to Knights of the Blind," 6, 37, 119–120, 123
Speeches, 77–120, 123
Story of My Life, 12, 13, 45, 48, 49–51, 59, 125, 126, 127, 128, 129, 136
"Strike Against War," 5, 29, 30, 36, 40, 41, 55, 99–103, 123, 136
Stringer, Tommy, 5, 24, 71, 75, 125, 140
Structural images, 33, 34

Stylistic devices, 29, 32

Suggestions for future research, 66–67

Sullivan, Anne, xxi, 3, 11, 12, 13, 14, 18–20, 24, 43, 45, 48–51, 52–53, 58–59, 68, 74, 75, 82, 106, 108, 111, 126, 127, 137, 138, 140, 143, 145, 148, 149

Swedenborg, Emanuel, 36, 65, 114, 128

Swedenborgianism, 6, 41, 68, 74, 114, 131, 148

Talking books, 72

Teacher: Anne Sullivan Macy, 13, 45, 125, 126, 127, 136

Teaching methods for blind and deaf pupils, 18–19

Theories of language, 20–21, 51–52, 62–63, 65–66, 67

Thomson, Polly, 3, 43

Tilney, Dr. Frederick, 35, 127

Transcendentalists, 65–66

Tuscumbia, Alabama, 2, 10, 131

Twain, Mark, 134, 139, 145

Typewriter, 22

Vaudeville Circuit, 6, 17, 22, 27, 43, 106–108, 123

"Victim" image, 49, 50–51, 68, 74

Villey, Pierre, 52, 127, 148

Voice of Helen Keller, 15

Volta Bureau, Library of the Alexander Graham Bell Association, xxiv, 7, 131, 138, 145

Wallace, Alfred Russell, 54, 95

War and peace images, 28–29, 33, 34, 99–103

Water pump, 10, 12, 20

Wells, H. G., 54, 95

West, Richard, xxiv

"What Is the IWW?" 126, 127

"Why I Became an IWW," 123, 138

Woman's suffrage, 23, 43, 118, 136, 137

Work Progress Administration, 72

The World I Live In, 55, 57, 125, 126, 128, 129, 137

Wright-Humason School for the Deaf, 14, 20

Writing speeches, 22

About the Author

LOIS J. EINHORN, Associate Professor of Rhetoric, at Binghamton University, has written at length on public address and rhetorical theory and criticism. She is the author of *Abraham Lincoln the Orator: Penetrating the Lincoln Legend* (Greenwood, 1992) and is co-author of *Effective Employment Interviewing: Unlocking Human Potential* (1982).

Great American Orators

Abraham Lincoln the Orator: Penetrating the Lincoln Legend
Lois J. Einhorn

Mark Twain: Protagonist for the Popular Culture
Marlene Boyd Vallin

Delightful Conviction: Jonathan Edwards and the Rhetoric of Conversion
Stephen R. Yarbrough and John C. Adams

Harry S. Truman: Presidential Rhetoric
Halford R. Ryan

Dwight D. Eisenhower: Strategic Communicator
Martin J. Medhurst

Ralph Waldo Emerson: Preacher and Lecturer
Lloyd Rohler

"In a Perilous Hour": The Public Address of John F. Kennedy
Steven R. Goldzwig and George N. Dionisopoulos

Douglas MacArthur: Warrior as Wordsmith
Bernard K. Duffy and Ronald H. Carpenter

Sojourner Truth as Orator: Wit, Story, and Song
Suzanne Pullon Fitch and Roseann M. Mandziuk

Frederick Douglass: Oratory from Slavery
David B. Chesebrough

Father Charles E. Coughlin: Surrogate Spokesperson for the Disaffected
Ronald H. Carpenter

Margaret Chase Smith: Model Public Servant
Marlene Boyd Vallin

ISBN 0-313-28643-4

HARDCOVER BAR CODE